INDIA PEACE OR WAR

INDIA PEACE OR WAR

C. S. RANGA IYER

GYAN

Published by

Gyan Publishing House
5, Ansari Road
Daryaganj, New Delhi-110002
Phone: 011-47034999, 9811692060
E-mail: books@gyanbooks.com

Distribution Network
gyanbooks.com
India, USA, Canada, UK, Australia

ISBN: 978-93-7225-283-5 (PB)

First Published, 1930

2nd Impression 2025

Printed at: Gyan Press, Delhi.

INDIA PEACE OR WAR
Author: C. S. RANGA IYER

INDIA
PEACE OR WAR?

INDIA
PEACE OR WAR?

BY

C. S. RANGA IYER

MEMBER OF THE INDIAN LEGISLATIVE ASSEMBLY
AUTHOR OF "FATHER INDIA" AND
"INDIA IN THE CRUCIBLE"

GEORGE G. HARRAP & CO. LTD.
LONDON BOMBAY SYDNEY

FOREWORD

INDIA loves peace, but not peace at any price. Her archers of yore drew their arrows to their heads. Her yeomen of the Middle Ages rode through blood. Less than eighty years ago her mutineers unsheathed the avenging sword. To-day a new India, nursed on the lap of Western science, is preparing for resistance as the West would prepare. Bayonets, she feels, are not so bad as chains.

"Break the chains, brave the bayonets, but keep the British connexion," say the elder statesmen. The advice is ignored. Young India has no use for a connexion which denies the pride of power. Without hesitation she sounds the trumpets and waves the standard. The combat thickens.

The Viceroy hurries to England to consult his Majesty's Government. His Excellency knows the limitations of the leaders. The pusillanimous *pundits* and *patels* are not made of the stuff of which heroes are made. The spirit of "either victory, or else a grave" does not animate them.

The Viceroy decided to tempt the leaders as Clive tempted Mir Jaffir, who won Bengal for the British *Raj*. Afraid of the rank and file, *pundit* and *patel* hummed and hawed. The moderates who started the fight swallowed the bait:

> He who fights and runs away
> May live to fight another day!

The bait was but a conference in Whitehall of Princes and politicians with the King's Ministers.

Politicians are a conceited tribe. They enjoy the music of their voices. A conference is a cheerful prospect. Resolutions will have to be moved; orations will have to be made. They bury the war-clubs and war-drums, and sing with the joy of children *Rule Britannia*.

INDIA—PEACE OR WAR?

Parliament is pleased. For the first time in its history all parties unite in sending a cheerful message to the Indian people. The message runs thus:

> That this House welcomes the evidence of the co-operation of Indian representatives in the settlement of the constitutional question, and relies upon the Government of India to encourage goodwill by the sympathetic conduct of its administrative and executive functions, particularly in relation to the expression of political opinion.

There was not a single dissentient voice. Socialist and Imperialist, Conservative and Radical, are happy. And their Anglicized friends in India say, "Salvation cannot come from within; it will come from Whitehall!"

The message, however, leaves Young India cold. She calls it the ancient trick of Clive, whose statue guards the gates of the India Office. Neither a Montagu nor a Benn dare unmake what Clive had made. The Conservative Viceroy will see to it. If he fails the steel frame of the Services will save him from the follies of his sympathy.

The thunder-roar of the Indian Congress is heard in London in Christmas week. It is no longer fearful. The united front in India is broken. The divided front in England is united again.

But are the British parties really united on the question of delaying Indian Home Rule? If they are, will this union last long? I venture to prophesy that Socialism will have to make Indian Home Rule its battle-cry, even as Gladstonian Liberalism took up the cause of Ireland in the last century. If no British party makes the Indian cause its own India will cease to draw inspiration from Britain.

My conversations with Socialist Ministers have convinced me that India need not seek isolation. Britain is her best friend. The Right Hon. J. R. Clynes, the Home Secretary, told me that not only Labour but all other parties in England mean to give India her due. Whether other parties play the game or not, the Socialists propose to repeat in India the successes they have achieved at The Hague, in Egypt, in America. India must know that they are only in office now. Even in office they have cleverly upset the apple-cart of Lords Reading and Birkenhead.

The most Imperialistic Viceroy and Secretary of State that ever set their hands to Indian affairs, Lord Reading and Lord Birkenhead, had inaugurated a policy to fulfil which the Simon Commission went out to India. In the midst of the Royal Commission's toil and turmoil a new policy was announced. His Majesty's Secretary of State for India proudly claimed that the Conservatives were opposed to his new move. The Liberals were opposed to it. And the Simon Commission was opposed to it. " And what did we do—we governed ! " The cheers from the Socialist benches, which did my heart good to witness from my place in the Dominions Gallery of the House of Commons, revealed that India had friends in a great and growing party in England. India, therefore, while pursuing her constitutional agitation, may abandon her programme of warlike preparations at home, and organize a tearing, raging propaganda in England. Educate the masters of Parliament.

An Indian debate in Parliament used to be the dullest thing in the world. The Right Hon. J. Ramsay MacDonald had made scores of speeches on Indian rights in his unregenerate days, but all to empty benches in the House of Commons. But on that historic day, November 7, 1929, the Prime Minister addressed a House which could not have been more crowded if Britain had declared war on India. And yet her representatives had met in Parliament to discuss what looked like a message of love—an innocent-looking message of peace.

The peace that India seeks is peace with honour :

> A peace is of the nature of a conquest ;
> For then both parties nobly are subdued,
> And neither party loser.

INDIA—PEACE OR WAR?

Is Shakespeare's England prepared to grant India that peace of which his Henry IV spoke? If so, let the Indo-British Conference in Whitehall sound the truce of God to the Eastern skies:

> As on the Sea of Galilee
> The Christ is whispering, "Peace."

India has had enough wars. Her warlike sons long to retire to some poetic nook and watch the ripening harvest. Will England let them bury the hatchet by applying to India the principles of her policy which has triumphed in the Colonies and the Dominions?

C. S. RANGA IYER

31 HAYMARKET, LONDON
January 1930

CONTENTS

PART I

INDIA UNDER BRITISH RULE

THE GROWTH OF LEGISLATURES—THE NATIONALIST MOVEMENT

CHAPTER I

PARLIAMENT AND INDIA

CHAPTER II

THE ADMINISTRATIVE MACHINE

CHAPTER III

THE TRIUMPH OF CONSTITUTIONALISM

INDIA—PEACE OR WAR?

CHAPTER IV

SIMLA—AND WHITEHALL

CHAPTER V

THE CONGRESS MOVEMENT

CHAPTER VI

GANDHI'S WAR ON REFORMS

CHAPTER VII

THE PROVINCIAL COUNCILS

CHAPTER VIII

PARTIES

CHAPTER XII

THE CLAMOUR OF THE PRINCES

CHAPTER XIII

AN INTRIGUING FUTURE

CHAPTER XIV

INDIA'S ULSTERS

CHAPTER XV

A DILEMMA?

CONTENTS

PART III

EVOLUTION OR REVOLUTION?

EXTREMISTS, TRUE AND FALSE—THE VICEROY SEPARATES THE SHEEP FROM THE GOATS

CHAPTER XVI

GANDHI—AND TERROR

CHAPTER XVII

THE DIPLOMAT AT WORK

CHAPTER XVIII

A TRIPARTITE CONFERENCE

CHAPTER XIX

THE VICEROY'S PROCLAMATION—AND AFTER

PAGE

CHAPTER XX

THE THREATENED REVOLT

CHAPTER XXI

INDIAN LEADERSHIP UNMASKED!

CHAPTER XXII

THE DANGER TO INDIA

POSTSCRIPT

PART I

INDIA UNDER BRITISH RULE

THE GROWTH OF THE LEGISLATURES—THE NATIONALIST MOVEMENT

CHAPTER I

PARLIAMENT AND INDIA

The reforms of 1919 did not inaugurate a new era, as has been hurriedly assumed by some Indian politicians, but gave tangible shape to the working of a principle—faint enough in the beginning—which dominated the constitutional development of Parliamentary government in England.

Modern England had its beginnings in the people's resistance to George III, who described politics as "a last resort of rascals"—a term of abuse for a large number of his subjects who were hostile to his methods of government. The loss of the American colonies which later came to be known as the United States created a new outlook in England in regard to her overseas territories.

Even before the American War of Independence the movement to liberalize the English constitution found expression through Blackstone and Burke. Burke's enthusiasm for Voltaire and Montesquieu was infectious. The popularity of Burke's fervid orations on Conciliation with America showed the new spirit which was animating public life in England.

In his Edmund Burke Bicentenary Commemoration Address (1928) at Trinity College, Dublin, Lord Birkenhead said that in the inception of the campaign against Warren Hastings there was no small degree of exaggeration, and in its development no small degree of extravagance, but there lay behind it one who was most deeply and closely moved by the spectacle of helpless and defenceless suffering. It was entirely right, opined Lord Birkenhead, that Warren Hastings should have been acquitted; and yet it was entirely right that some of the happenings which formed the subject of the charges should, in the interests of humanity, and for the purpose of continuing the sacred charge incurred toward so many hundreds of millions of helpless Indians, have been examined.

The Regulating Act of 1773 and Pitt's Act of 1784 relating to India were passed at a time when there was a great awakening of the public conscience in England, when more attention began to be paid by her to her far-flung Dominions and dependencies.

The Indian sceptic reads in these Acts the enlightened self-interest of England, and not a desire in her to create the democratic institutions of a future date. But even the most sceptical and the least generous of critics cannot deny the effect in India, however remote, of the Liberal upheaval in England. This is discernible in the Charter Act of 1833, which is a reflex of the democratic progress in England, which crystallized in the Parliamentary reforms of 1832.

It may be urged by the critic that the Parliamentary reforms of 1832 gave so much to England and the Charter Act of 1833 so little to India. The forces which were at work in England were absent in India, and therefore it was natural that India should not share these benefits to the same degree as England, but undeniably the new reforms in England had their repercussions in India.

England derived from the New Model Parliament benefits such as the Poor Law of 1834, which brought untold relief to the working classes, and the municipal reforms, which made local self-government a reality. To India the first reformed Parliament gave the Charter Act of 1833. And throughout the Empire, in the same year, slavery was abolished, thanks to Wilberforce and the Evangelicals, whose parish was the world and whose constituency was humanity.

The spirit of equality, fraternity, and humanity which animated the liberation of the slaves within the British Empire also inspired the Act of 1833. It anticipated the

Queen's proclamation of 1858. The Charter Act laid it down that

> No native of the said territories shall by reason only of his religion, place of birth, descent, colour, or any of them, be debarred from holding any place, office, or employment under the Company.

This strong and clear declaration of equality of status and opportunity, be the King's subjects Indian or British, was worthy of the new faith in democracy which had come to dwell in old England. No better apostle of that faith could there be than Macaulay, who threw open to India the flood-gates of Western education in his famous minute of February 2, 1835. India's contact with the main stream of the world's thought and learning was bound to change her face and outlook. That was Macaulay's set purpose. That was England's mission in India.

With Western education came Western ideas of liberty and a desire for Parliamentary institutions, which Western writers described as "the Indian unrest." The Indian National movement came into existence, and found a medium for its expression in the Indian National Congress.

The history of the Congress is briefly surveyed in another chapter, as it is the history of the evolution of India's nationalism and self-assertion. Suffice it to say that the birth of the Congress coincided with the new Liberal spirit which found powerful expression in England. In 1880 Gladstone came into power, and interested himself in the political progress of India as no Prime Minister before him had done. "Our title to be in India," said Gladstone, "depends on a first condition, that our being there is profitable to the Indian nations; and on a second condition, that we can make them see and understand it to be profitable."

After the famous "Midlothian" election campaign, when Gladstone defeated Disraeli, Lord Lytton, who was a Conservative, resigned his Viceroyalty. Gladstone appointed as his successor Lord Ripon, who was steeped in the spirit of Liberalism.

Lord Lytton's Viceroyalty had created in India acute disappointment. Instead of conciliating the educated classes, who had expected that they would be given a larger share in the administration of their country, Lord Lytton had passed repressive laws to suppress the Press and platform. He was carrying out the Imperialist policy of Disraeli.

Lord Lytton himself had cynically described his Indian policy in words which, when they received unexpected publicity in India, surprised the Indian public. " We all know that their claims and expectations," he wrote, referring to those based by Indians on the Queen's pledges, " never can or will be fulfilled. We have to choose between prohibiting them and cheating them, and we have chosen the [less] straightforward course." [1]

Lord Lytton himself had no doubt in his own mind that both the Governments of India and England were " unable to answer satisfactorily the charge of having taken every means in their power of breaking to the heart the words of promise uttered to the ear." [2]

Lord Lytton's resignation was hailed with relief in India. The coming of Gladstone to power was a guarantee of liberal reforms to the educated classes, who took a real interest in British politics.

Lord Ripon's announcement of his reform policy revealed to the Indian mind that the realization of Indian aspirations would advance *pari passu* with the progress of public opinion in England. As the Romans of old were proud to say, " *Civis Romanus sum*," so the Indian Nationalist of those days was proud to boast that he belonged to an Empire which held aloft the banner of freedom, an Empire whose citizens might justly boast, " *Civis Britannicus sum*." If one reads the speeches of Sir Surendranath Bannerjee, Dadabhai Naoroji, and other early nation-builders one finds this

[1] *India*, by Sir Valentine Chirol, p. 85. [2] *Ibid.*

enthusiasm for the Empire and Britain and the mother of Parliaments.

Lord Ripon's reforming zeal met with angry opposition from the British community, who especially succeeded in thwarting the plans and purpose of the Ilbert Bill. This organized opposition of the European non-official community in India, who had the implicit and sometimes explicit support of the officials, revealed to the Indian mind that, however progressive and liberal, however well-intentioned and noble, the British Government or the particular party in power might be, India could not expect anything satisfactory until and unless her educated middle classes were organized and united and had an organ of their own.

The failure of Lord Ripon gave India the Indian National Congress. The strength of the Congress increased with the spread of education—especially secondary and higher education—among the middle classes. This progress of thought in India coincided with the rapid increase of the power of Parliament in England. Educated India, which had watched the vast progress of Parliamentary reforms in England, aspired for the same for herself.

A study of the State Papers relating to the discussion which preceded the Indian Council Act of 1892 would reveal how Parliament decided to extend to India the principle of election, guarded though it was with restrictions and limitations. The application of the elective principle could not be denied for long to a people who, in Lord Curzon's words, were "feeding their minds on a Western diet," which had raised "entire sections of the community from torpor to life, and lifted India on to a higher moral plane." [1]

The reaction of British political progress on India became more pronounced and irresistible with the eating up of space and time by scientific inventions and the opening of the Suez Canal.

The return of the Liberals to power in 1905 and the grant

[1] *The Place of India in the Empire*, by Lord Curzon, p. 38.

of Dominion status in 1907 to the Transvaal paved the road for the Morley-Minto reforms. In this connexion it may be noted that the manner in which the Transvaal secured admission to Dominion status brought into existence the Extremist Party in India, the leaders of which said that freedom could not be secured by eloquence, but only by violence. Propaganda on these lines created the revolutionary movement in India.

However that may be, the Morley-Minto reforms resemble in many essential respects the constitution of the self-governing colonies before they were endowed with Dominion status. The representatives of the people were associated in the work of legislation so far as possible without impairing the power of the Executive, who were to be in control of the administration. The Morley-Minto reforms made the Montagu-Chelmsford reforms inevitable.

There are some who even at this date say that the Montagu reforms were conceived in ignorance and carried out in haste through an indifferent Parliament. Even a well-informed critic of the reputation of Sir Leslie Scott gave expression to the view that " the late Mr Montagu forced on a suspicious House of Commons the Montagu-Chelmsford constitutional reforms in British India."

Lord Ronaldshay, who had a hand in working the reforms as the Governor of Bengal and unique opportunities of studying the inception of the reforms, has placed it on record that it was not Mr Montagu who forced the reforms, but the forces which had been let loose, the ideals which found vent, and the aspirations which had been formulated during the War which had dragged India, with the rest of the world, through the track of centuries. In fairness to the House of Commons it must be said that it supported Mr Montagu, who, in his concluding speech on the Bill, said :

> It is a great thing for the history of India that the House of Commons has given this Bill, up to this stage, a spirit of almost complete, if not complete, unanimity, neither snatching a little

more here nor saving a little more there, but giving it generously and with a set purpose that this shall be a transitional constitution on a road which the House of Commons will to-day determine to follow.

Mr Montagu's statement was endorsed by an eyewitness, the reporter of *The Times*, who noted that when the Bill passed the third reading the cheers in the House were charged with real emotion. "It was a Bill," wrote this observer, "worthy both of Britain and of India, and the debates were informed with a high seriousness, and a sense that history was in the making."

If the spirit which animated Parliament was one of real enthusiasm, which was noticed by all observers, when the Reforms Bill was passed, right from the beginning every care was taken that extravagant promises too difficult to fulfil were not held out to India. The formula which pledged the progressive development of responsible government was as carefully examined by the Cabinet as the Montagu-Chelmsford Report was by the Joint Parliamentary Committee, and the Reforms Bill itself by the House of Commons. In fact, from first to last the best brains in both Houses of Parliament had given anxious attention to it.

The origin of the announcement of August 1917 was Simla-Delhi and not Whitehall. Much credit is due in this respect to Lord Chelmsford and his Cabinet, and to that veteran statesman, Sir Chettur Sankaran Nair, who was said to have inspired the "Nineteeners' Memorandum"—so christened after the nineteen signatories who were members of the Indian Legislative Council, the leading spirits of which were Bhupendranath Basu and Surendranath Bannerjee—which subsequently became the basis for the Joint Scheme of the Indian National Congress and the All India Muslim League. *The Madras Mail*, an organ of the European community, denounced Sir Chettur Sankaran Nair as the "emasculator-in-chief" of the Government of India, but subsequent events have conclusively proved that the Radical statesman of Malabar was a tower of strength to the Government in troublous times, even as he was its beacon when it was naturally doubting the wisdom of a strong line of action.

The Viceroy and his Council unanimously pressed on the Secretary of State for India, Mr (now Sir) Austen Chamberlain, the need for an announcement containing the views and intentions of his Majesty's Government in regard to India.

In May 1917 Mr Chamberlain, the Secretary of State for India, invited the attention of his colleagues to the Indian problem, in a letter in which he wrote that "upon a right decision at that critical time depended the peace and contentment of India for years and perhaps for generations to come."[1]

Mr Chamberlain left the Government in July as a result of the Mesopotamia Commission Report. Mr Montagu, who succeeded him, worked upon Mr Chamberlain's plans.

Views have been expressed by certain writers on India that the reforms were given as a reward for India's part in the War. Those who say that the reforms were a reward for India's part in the War do England little justice. This criticism has been answered by as high an authority as Lord Curzon himself. India did not serve in the War in the expectation of rewards to come. As well might one who pretends that India was blessed with far-reaching reforms as reward speak of a midwife having presented the lady on whom she attended with an adult child, for it must be noted that the Montagu scheme marked the half-way house between responsible government and government carried on with the advice of the Legislature. It was not the beginning of legislative reforms in India, but a fair stage in their growth.

Lord Ronaldshay says in his *Life of Lord Curzon* that the need for a further step forward arose neither because the War justified it nor because experience demanded it, but

[1] *Life of Lord Curzon*, by Lord Ronaldshay, vol. iii, p. 162.

because, as Lord Curzon wrote to the War Cabinet in June 1917, " we are expected to translate into practice in our own domestic household the sentiments which we have so enthusiastically preached."

The outlook of Parliament was widened by the War, and this widening of the outlook extended to the Conservatives and Liberals. Even Lord Curzon recognized the necessity of making a promise to India in keeping with the spirit of the day.

Mr Montagu submitted to the Cabinet the following formula :

> His Majesty's Government and the Government of India have in view the gradual development of free institutions in India with a view to ultimate self-government within the Empire.

Mr Montagu was cautious. He had to carry the Conservatives with him. He did not specify the type of self-governing institutions to be set up in India. Whether the Executive should be responsible to and therefore removable by the Legislature were matters which he left open. But Lord Curzon made the goal of India and the type of free institutions specific when he redrafted the pronouncement on the eve of its publication as follows :

> The policy of his Majesty's Government, with which the Government of India are in complete accord, is that of the increasing association of Indians in every branch of the administration and the gradual development of self-governing institutions with a view to the progressive realization of responsible government in India as an integral part of the British Empire.

" When we came to the constitutional question," Lord Curzon wrote in a letter to Mr Chamberlain, whose formula Mr Montagu had adopted, " I suggested a new formula which seemed to me rather safer and certainly nearer to my own point of view than the words you had originally favoured—namely, self-government." [1] In a subsequent letter to the Viceroy Lord Curzon admitted "indeed, the actual words were mine."

Lord Ronaldshay tells us that Lord Curzon's introduction of the words "responsible government" instead of "self-government" can only have meant that it was a Parliamentary system which Britain aimed at setting up in India. It would appear that the wording was suggested to Lord Curzon by a lecture on the "Problems of Indian Government," delivered by Lord Islington at the request of the Oxford Delegacy for the Extension of University Teaching, in which the importance of the expression "responsible self-government" was fully interpreted. The lecture was delivered on August 8, 1917, and a copy of it presented by the author to Lord Curzon a day or two before the latter changed Mr Montagu's formula. It is significant that Lord Curzon, who had been reading the lecture, underlined in pencil two passages which may be quoted:

> I would say at once that, if the ideals of the British Empire stand for anything, India's future must be in accord with those ideals, and her ultimate ambition, which she must one day realize, after successfully surmounting the difficulties before her, is the attainment of responsible government within the Empire. . . . It is to be remembered that if, in deference to the Legislative Council, the Government modify their policy, the Council would have to shoulder the responsibility for the results. This is the essence of responsible government as we understand it. To secure its introduction into Indian Local Government a suitable system of elections is important, so that the elected

[1] Sir Malcolm Hailey, as Home Member of the Government of India, emphasized the distinction between "self-government" and "responsible government" in his speech in the Legislative Assembly on February 8, 1924. The report of the so-called Indian All Parties Conference published in 1928 challenged the accuracy of Sir Malcolm's interpretation. This report naïvely says: "The speech may be taken to be the beginning of a new current of thought in official circles in India." Sir Malcolm Hailey, however, had obviously based his observations on his inner knowledge of differences in the British Cabinet in regard to the formula, since disclosed in Lord Ronaldshay's *Life of Lord Curzon*, vol. iii, pp. 162–176, published in 1928.

members may be properly representative of the various classes of Indian society. Only if this is done will it be possible, consistently with the interests of the people, to make them realize that for whatever they say or do they will be held accountable to constituents free to displace them if they fail to give satisfaction.[1]

We need not further labour the point that the British Government aimed in India at the establishment of Parliamentary constitutions such as existed in England. That even the Congress politicians did not ask for responsible government, but self-government, was known to those who had read the Congress League Scheme, which was submitted to Mr Montagu and Lord Chelmsford. Even as the Cabinet had carefully scrutinized the language of England's pledge to India, Parliament devoted considerable time to the examination of the Montagu-Chelmsford Report.

That there were prophets of pessimism could not have surprised the student of Imperial history who knew that much apprehension and feelings of disgust found expression in high quarters when responsible government was granted to Canada in the forties of the last century. Disraeli spoke of "those wretched colonies," hanging "like a millstone round our neck." When Parliament's pronouncement was published in August 1917, both in India and England wise men hailed it as a noble achievement of statesmanship.

The same spirit which produced the Canada Bill of 1840 and the South African settlement of 1907 was also responsible for England's decision to grant India Dominion status. That Mr Montagu's scheme was superior to the Congress League draft is conclusively established by the fact that those who were responsible for the latter enthusiastically settled down to work the former.

The reforms of 1919 were the logical outcome of the growth of the Legislature, and of the spirit of progressive realization of responsible government which had been at

[1] *Life of Lord Curzon*, vol. iii, pp. 168–169.

work in Indian politics, however dim and feeble at the beginning, from 1833.

The question with which the British Parliament was face to face in 1919 was this: Was the discontent of the educated classes to be increased an hundredfold by the refusal to grant timely concessions, or was Indian friendship to be cultivated and improved by resorting to the same methods which gave England democracy and the Colonies responsible government?

India, it must be remembered, was no longer isolated from the world, which had considerably shrunk. The Western monopoly in ideas had become a thing of the past. Time and world forces had been shaping India's destiny since 1858. A large number of Indian students had gone to the universities of Europe and America. American and European literature was pouring into India. There could be no better proof that large reforms could no longer be delayed than that a cautious statesman like Lord Curzon should have defended in the House of Lords, where the reforms had more opponents than in the Commons, the forward policy of the Coalition Government when the Indian Reforms Bill came up for second reading on December 12, 1919. Though Lord Curzon did not think that India would be better governed under the new dispensation than it had been in the past, though he feared that the standard would tend to fall, at the same time he realized that with

> the modern ideal of Nationalism and self-determination making in the circumstances of the times so strong an appeal, the peoples of countries such as India attached much more importance to being governed, even though not so well-governed, by themselves, than they did to being even superbly governed by another race.[1]

The surging tide of national feeling which was the principal feature of the nineteenth century in Europe became Asia's

[1] *Life of Lord Curzon*, vol. iii, p. 176.

in the twentieth. Japan's triumph against Russia heralded the dawn of a new age in the East. And the dispatch of Indian troops to the battlefields of Europe revealed as with a flash that India's claim to a place in the comity of nations as an equal member was irresistible.

CHAPTER II

THE ADMINISTRATIVE MACHINE

British India, which comprises that part of the great Indian Empire which is directly under British rule, is governed according to various Parliamentary statutes which are now consolidated in the Government of India Act, 1915, as amended by the Government of India (Amendment) Act, 1916, the Government of India Act, 1919, and the Government of India (Leave of Absence) Act, 1924. The British Crown is the repository of all power. All powers are exercised in its name. All revenues, tributes, and other payments are received in his Majesty's name and disposed of for purposes of the Government of India.

Thanks to Disraeli, the great Jewish Prime Minister, and his loyal devotion to Queen Victoria, the Queen of England came to be known as the Empress of India. Under the Royal Titles Act of 1876 England's King is also India's Emperor.

The Government of India is vested in the Governor-General in Council. They are jointly responsible for the superintendence, direction, and control of the civil and military administration of the country. The first Governor-General was Warren Hastings (1774), immortalized by his impeachment by the great Irish statesman Edmund Burke. The last Governor-General, so far as this book is concerned, is Baron Irwin of Kirby Underdale, P.C., who took office in April 1926.

Warren Hastings was really the Governor-General of Fort William in Bengal. Until 1834 there were no Governor-Generals of India. Since 1858, when the Government of India was transferred from the East India Company to the Crown, the Governor-General also became the Viceroy.

The Governor-General and Viceroy is appointed by the Crown. He holds his office for five years. He draws an annual salary of Rs. 256,000. Directly under the Governor-General is the Foreign and Political Department, which deals with foreign affairs and the Indian States.

Above the Governor-General in Council is the Secretary of State for India, whose salary and the cost of the India Office for other than agency services are borne not by the Indian Exchequer, as before the reforms of 1919, but by the British Exchequer. This was one of the achievements of the late Edwin Montagu's statesmanship. The Secretary of State for India is assisted by a Council. This Council generally consists of not less than eight members, and not more than twelve. The Secretary of State himself appoints them for a term of five years. One-half of the members of the India Council must be persons who have served or resided ten years in India, and who have not left that country more than five years prior to their appointment.

A Member of the India Council may be removed by his Majesty upon an address from both the House of Commons and the House of Lords. On the removal of the Member the Secretary of State may, for special reasons recorded in a minute signed by him and placed before both Houses of Parliament, reappoint a Member of the Council for a further term of five years. Unlike the Members of the Viceroy's Executive Council, those of the India Council cannot sit in Parliament. The latter differs from the former in another fundamental respect. The India Council in London has no power of initiative or administrative authority.[1] It is only an advisory body. The Nationalists have repeatedly demanded the abolition of the India Council, which they denounce as an " asylum of fossilized bureaucrats."

Be that as it may, the duties of the Council of the Secretary

[1] In a letter to the present writer a high English official—indisputably the clearest legal brain to-day of the Government of India—describes the India Council as " that effete and moribund body " !

of State for India are to assist in the conducting of the business transacted in the United Kingdom in relation to the Government of India.

The power of the Secretary of State is enormous. A strong Secretary of State can ignore his Council. He seldom consults it before initiating big schemes fraught with serious results. He can also turn down the suggestions of the Viceroy and his Executive Council. For instance, we have the example of a dominating Secretary of State like Lord Morley, who imposed his will on Lord Minto in regard to his reform policy.[1] We have again the instance of another dominating Secretary of State, Lord Birkenhead, who forced Lord Irwin to abandon his original idea of a mixed Commission of Indians and Europeans to investigate the working of the reforms. It was the opinion in well-informed circles that if only Lord Irwin could have had his way the blunder of excluding Indians from the Statutory Commission, presided over by Sir John Simon, would not have occurred. This blunder was recognized by all right-thinking Englishmen. It has been repaired by the decision to summon an Indian Conference in Whitehall.[2]

However that may be, subject to the Government of India Act and Rules made thereunder, the Secretary of State in Council controls the expenditure of the revenues of India both in India and elsewhere, and no appropriation can be made without the concurrence of the majority votes in the Council. The Secretary of State regulates the transactions of business.

The interference of the Secretary of State with the Government of India, however, is less frequent than in the past on matters of daily routine and administration, though not essential policy.

The introduction of a Legislative Assembly in India with a large elected majority has rendered it desirable that the

[1] *Recollections*, by Lord Morley, vol. ii.
[2] The Viceroy's Proclamation of November 1929.

Secretary of State for India should interfere only in exceptional circumstances in matters of purely Indian interest where the Government of India and the Legislature in India are in agreement.

The Indian Legislature consists of the Governor-General and two Chambers—the Council of State and the Legislative Assembly—which were inaugurated in 1921 by his Royal Highness the Duke of Connaught. The Council of State has 60 members; of them 33 are elected and 27 nominated. Twenty of these nominated members may be officials, but not more than 17 officials are nominated at present. The Assembly consists of 145 members, of whom 104 are elected and 41 nominated, of whom 26 are to be officials. The Council of State is dissolved on the expiry of five years, whereas the life of the Assembly is only three years. The Governor-General has, for special reasons, the power of extending their period or dissolving them earlier.

Under the Government of India Act joint sittings of the Council of State and the Legislative Assembly may be held for settlement of differences between them. Such a joint session has never been held, though differences between them have constantly arisen.

The Legislative Assembly was presided over for the first four years by a President nominated by the Governor-General. After the nominated President came the era of an elected President.

The Central Legislature—namely, the Council of State and the Assembly—has the power, subject, of course, to restrictions, to make laws for all persons within British India and for Indian subjects of his Majesty.

From this it should not be imagined that the Central Legislature is endowed with the power of Parliament. It is no more and no less than an advisory body. It has no power of initiative. It has only the power of speech.

The real power is in the Governor-General, who, with the assent of his Majesty signified, after copies of the proposed enactment are laid before both Houses of the British Parliament, may pass measures essential for the safety, tranquillity, or interest of British India or any part thereof in the teeth of opposition alike from the Legislative Assembly and the Council of State.

The power of Parliament is therefore supreme. Thus the Government of India—notwithstanding the fact that the Legislative Assembly is drawn from a large electorate and has a large majority—is responsible under the constitution to his Majesty's Government, who are responsible to the British electorate.

This state of affairs has been galling to the democratic spirit of the politically minded classes in India, who demand that responsibility should be transferred from the British to the Indian electorate. The Government of India themselves have experienced, during the period of the reforms, the inconvenience and embarrassment of carrying on the administration with a Legislature in which they are only a small minority.

The Members of the Governor-General's Executive Council, who are appointed by the Crown for a term of five years, are six in number, with a salary of Rs. 80,000 a year each. They have charge of the following portfolios: Home; Finance; Education, Health and Lands; Law; Railways, Commerce and Ecclesiastical; Industries and Labour.

The Commander-in-Chief is also the Army Member of the Executive Council of the Viceroy. There is a growing feeling among the non-official Indian Members that a separate Army Member should be appointed who will be in charge of the Military Portfolio and represent the Government of India in the Legislature.

The Government of India Act, 1919, effected important rearrangements in the provincial sphere, the government of which had hitherto been carried on as a united whole, but was henceforward divided between the Governor acting with the Executive Council and the Governor acting with his

Ministers. The Devolution Rules under the 1919 Act classify the various functions of Government as Central and Provincial. The Central subjects are military and foreign affairs, tariffs and customs, railways, posts and telegraphs, income-tax, currency and the public duty, commerce and shipping, and legislation relating to civil and criminal law. These subjects are by their very nature those which cannot be administered by a Provincial Government. For purposes of convenience certain subjects, such as the collection of income-tax, are dealt with by the Provincial Governments as the agents of the Central Government.

The Provincial Administration is divided into Reserved and Transferred Departments, and is responsible to two authorities. The Crown nominates the 'Reserved' half, as it is called, which consists of the Governor and his Executive Councillors. The Transferred half is selected from among the Members of the Provincial Legislature by the Governor. The Reserved subjects are administered by the Provincial Governments, subject to the unimpaired powers of control of the Governor-General in Council. The interference of the Governor-General in Council in the administration of the Transferred Department is restricted only where it is necessary to safeguard Central subjects, or to settle matters of dispute between two or more provinces, or to safeguard the due exercise and performance of any powers and duties possessed by or imposed on the Governor-General in Council in regard to the High Commissioner, to the raising of loans by the local Governments, or to under-rules made by the Secretary of State in Council. The Transferred subjects, which are under the control of Indian Ministers, with certain reservations, include local self-government, medical administration, public health and sanitation, education, public works, except irrigation, agriculture, fisheries, co-operative societies, excise, registration, development of industries, adulteration, weights and measures, and religious and charitable endowments.

The Transferred subjects are not the same in all the provinces; for instance, in one or two provinces forests are transferred to the control of the Indian Ministers, whereas in other provinces they are not.

The most important of the Reserved subjects are police, law and order, land revenue, and irrigation and forests in the majority of the provinces.

The Indian public demand the abolition of dyarchy in the provinces. They want complete control of the provincial administration by the Provincial Legislature. This demand has the entire support of Moderates, Conservatives, and Radicals.

The first charge on the revenues of the provinces is the contribution to the Central Government of certain annual sums.

The Governor's Executive Council consists usually of four members appointed by the Crown, one having a qualification of twelve years' public service in India.

The Provincial Legislature consists only of a single Chamber at present, though the introduction of a double Chamber system in the spacious days of the future seems likely. The Provincial Legislature has an elected non-official majority—70 per cent. in British India and 60 per cent. in Burma. It contains not more than 20 per cent. of official members; the remaining percentage is made up of nominations and special representations. The Provincial Legislature has the power to vote all expenditure which is subject to certain specified exceptions.

The local Government is omnipotent so far as the incurring of expenditure relating to Reserved subjects is concerned. Without the assent of the Council the Governor has the power to certify a certain expenditure to be necessary.

The Provincial Legislature's life, like that of the Legislative Assembly, is only three years; but the Governor has the power of dissolving it earlier or extending its period for one year.

Under the system of dyarchy the Ministers cannot be members of the permanent Services, unless they happen to be retired members elected to the Legislature. The Governor is not a Member of the Legislative Council, but addresses the same. The provinces in which dyarchy has been introduced are Madras, Bombay, Bengal, the Punjab, Assam, the United Provinces, Burma, the Central Provinces, and Bihar and Orissa. In the first seven provinces the franchise has been extended also to women. Women are also eligible for the membership of Councils in the Madras and Bombay Presidencies and, through constituencies therein, for the Legislative Assembly. There is as yet no woman Member of the Legislative Assembly.

The number of members of the Provincial Legislatures varies in each province, as shown in the statement below:

Names of Provinces	Area in Square Miles in 1921	Population in 1921	Number of Members in the Legislatures
Madras Presidency	142,260	42,318,985	118
Bombay Presidency	123,621	19,348,219	111
Bengal	76,843	46,695,536	125
United Provinces	106,295	45,375,787	118
Punjab	99,846	20,685,024	83
Bihar and Orissa	83,161	34,002,189	98
Central Provinces and Berar	99,876	13,912,760	70
Assam	53,015	7,606,230	53
Burma	233,707	13,212,192	92

A Legislative Council has also been formed for Coorg, which is a small province with an area of 1582 square miles and a population of 163,838.

Principal among the smaller provinces, which do not possess Legislative Councils, is the North-West Frontier Province, which has an area of 13,419 square miles and a population of 2,251,340. The Muslims of India have almost with one voice demanded the extension to the North-West Frontier Province of the benefit of the 1919 reforms.

The Government, however, have so far delayed the taking of that measure, because they have presumably been swayed by frontier considerations which are peculiar to India.

A word must be said of the small administrative units. The Province of Delhi, the smallest in India, has a population of 488,188 and an area of 593 square miles. The Province of Baluchistan has an area of 54,228 square miles and a population of 420,648. The Andamans and Nicobars have an area of 3143 square miles and a population of 27,086. Ajmere-Merwara is an Agency Tract which the British resumed after the Pindari War in 1818. It is administered by a Chief Commissioner, who is also the Agent to the Governor-General in Rajputana. The local administration is under a Commissioner. It has a population of 495,271 and an area of 2711 square miles.

The Andaman Islands, which had been used since 1858 by the Government of India as a penal settlement for life and long-term convicts, are in charge of a Chief Commissioner under the Government of India. The Nicobar Islands, situated to the south of the Andamans, where the occupation of the people is the coconut trade, which they have been carrying on for the last 1500 years, and whose coconut production is estimated at 15,000,000 nuts per annum, are administered by a permanent Assistant Commissioner and a *tahsildar*, and attached to the Chief Commissionership of the Andamans and Nicobars.

In Baluchistan the head of the Civil Administration is the Agent to the Governor-General and Chief Commissioner.

The Delhi Province, formerly a part of the Punjab, was constituted in 1912 as a separate province under a Chief Commissioner. There is an idea, which the Government have not acknowledged in replies to numerous interpellations from Members of the Central Legislature, of expanding the Delhi Province at the expense of the western districts of the United Provinces and south-eastern districts of the Punjab in the neighbourhood of Delhi. The idea is an excellent one.

CHAPTER III

THE TRIUMPH OF CONSTITUTIONALISM

THE Legislative Assembly began its career at a time when the Montagu-Chelmsford reforms had more enemies than friends in India. But the manner in which the reforms were worked induced the detractors thereof to abandon their policy of boycott and non-co-operation. The most vociferous and violent of the boycotters at the time—but since the first elected President of the Assembly, trying to work the reforms as best as he could—made a remarkable confession to the effect that the working of the Assembly under the guidance of Sir Frederick Whyte had induced him to abandon the wild-goose chase of non-co-operation.[1]

A study of the first session of the Assembly, terminating on March 29, 1921, and consisting entirely of politicians who believed in the reforms, would show how a new spirit had come to dwell in India—a spirit which grew stronger in subsequent sessions, until it began to exercise a powerful influence on those who three years later came to wreck the constitution, but remained to work it—a spirit which showed itself in the Assembly's willingness to render every assistance to carry on the King's Government, while resolutely determined to wrest from the hands of the Executive whatever powers it could and add them to its own armoury. Already it was noticeable how the Assembly began to display that factiousness which politics invariably develop; yet its general attitude so far as the Government was concerned was indeed moderate and its tone courteous.

The Assembly tried to fulfil the principal function of a critical Parliament, which is the grand inquest of the nation

[1] *Proceedings of the Legislative Assembly*, August 1925.

into all that affects the vital well-being of the masses and individuals alike, scrupulously and courageously demanding that the Government should explain and justify their acts. On the constructive side its endeavours might have been feebler, but it was inevitable so long as it remained only an advisory body, and so long as the Opposition was not invited to shoulder the burdens of administration.

The discussion on the Budget, both railway and general, and the proceedings connected with the appointment of the Standing Finance Committee and the Committee on Public Accounts, apart from the outstanding debates on resolutions moved in the first, second, and third Assembly, were primarily political. In the first Assembly the debates related to such sensational questions as the administration of martial law in the Punjab, the Esher proposals regarding the Army in India, the Press Act, the Nankana tragedy, which showed as by a searchlight the growing discontent among the Sikhs regarding their religious institutions, and the non-co-operation movement, on the last of which the Legislature gave absolute support to the Government, thus fulfilling the essential function of upholding the law and maintaining order. The Punjab resolution asked the Government:

1. To declare its adhesion to the principle of equal partnership for Indian and European in the British Empire.

2. To express regret that martial law in the Punjab violated this fundamental Imperial principle.

3. To administer deterrent punishment to officers guilty of an improper exercise of their powers, including the withdrawal of their pensions.

4. To assure itself that adequate compensation is awarded to those who lost their relatives at Jallianwala Bagh and elsewhere.

One striking feature of the debate was the solicitude of the Government and the Opposition alike to observe moderation in language and criticism. By the Government's accepting the third clause, which demanded the deterrent punishment of offenders, it was possible to adopt a unanimous resolution, thanks to the sense of statesmanship of the new Parliamentarians. The moderation and statesmanship and sweet reasonableness of the loyal Members of the first Legislative Assembly could not have achieved a greater triumph or a more brilliant conquest than the seduction of the erstwhile non-co-operators to the Legislatures and their subsequent alliance with the very Moderates whom they had cursed with bell, book, and candle as having sold their soul for a mess of pottage.

The Assembly by its compromise on the Punjab problem —on which the non-co-operation movement out in the country was founded—justified its uncompromising plea for co-operation. In the words of the mover of that resolution, the Assembly accepted it in a spirit which agreed to throw the past behind them, and to go forward together to "fulfil his Royal Highness's desire 'to forgive where we have to forgive, and to join hands and to work together to realize the hopes that arise from to-day.'" [1]

The debate on the Press Act, which followed a week later, disclosed that the new Members of the Legislative Assembly did not want to repeal it, but only to modify it. They were for imposing certain restrictions on the Press! The Government, who were naturally willing to meet the non-officials half-way, moved for the appointment of a committee to examine the Press and Registration of Books Act, 1867, and the Indian Press Act, 1910, and report what modifications were required in the existing law. The discussion resulted in a compromise, which was embodied in an agreed proposition, which may be quoted:

> This Assembly recommends to the Governor-General in Council that a committee, of whom not less than two-thirds shall be non-officials, be appointed to examine the Press and Registration of Books Act, 1867, the Newspaper Incitement Act (VII) of 1908, and the Indian Press Act, 1910, and to

[1] *Legislative Assembly Proceedings*, February 1921.

report which of these should be repealed or modified, and, in the latter case, what modifications are required.

The importance of this compromise will be clear only to those who understand that the Government have clearly felt that the Press Act was a necessary instrument for the combating of seditious propaganda. The Government have always maintained that scandalous libel, barely concealed incitements to violence, malevolent perversion of Government activity, and appeals to the basest human passions are the stock-in-trade of the reptile organs whose influence over an unlearned community is as vast as it is mischievous. The people's representative, on the other hand, has invariably urged that the ordinary law of the land was strong enough to prevent the spread of sedition and to suppress dangerous newspapers. The opposition of these newspapers to the continuance of the Press Act on the Statute Book is based on its abuse by an executive which owes no responsibility to the people, and which cannot bear harsh and persistent nationalist propaganda. The Government's reasonableness led at a later stage to the repeal of the Press Act, which revealed to the non-co-operators the virtue and value of fruitful co-operation.

The Esher Report debate resulted in the appointment of a committee, with Lord Esher at its head, to inquire into the Indian military system. Its terms of reference included an examination of the Indian Army's relations with the War Office and the India Office; and its report, published in October 1920, contained some matter which was calculated to arouse suspicion in India that the Indian Army might be used for Imperial purposes against the wishes of the Indian people. A non-official Member of the Assembly therefore moved a resolution on February 17 to the effect that

the Army in India should be entirely under the control, real as well as nominal, of the Government of India, and should be free from any domination or interference by the War

Office on matters of military policy—and that such co-ordination as may be desirable between the military policies or organizations of different parts of the Empire should be secured by discussion and agreement at conferences at which India is adequately represented.

Though the original resolution was modified as a result of the debate thereon, the amendment which was adopted recommended to the Governor-General in Council that the Army in India should be entirely under the control of the Government of India, and a Committee of the House was subsequently formed to consider the Esher Committee's Report and to make recommendations. Its conclusions were forwarded to his Majesty's Government in Great Britain for examination by a sub-committee of the Committee of Imperial Defence. When the Swarajists were allured into the Councils by this constructive endeavour three years later they profusely quoted from the Esher Committee's proposals, and eventually succeeded in securing the appointment of the Skeen Committee, whose purpose, among others, was to inquire into the question of the establishment of a military college in India. It is interesting to note that the leader of the Swaraj Party himself happily agreed to serve on that committee, though the intransigents of the Congress, much to his regret, caused him to withdraw from it in the middle of his labours.

During the first Budget discussion under the new reforms our representatives showed a real sense of responsibility. The Budget showed a deficit of over one hundred and eighty millions of rupees. The non-official members concentrated their attention on the actual taxes by which the deficit would be wiped out; they did not resort to the tactics of refusing all proposed taxation, as well as many grants for ordinary administrative charges. The Assembly had the power to do so. The Swarajists soon after their Council entry attempted this, but, realizing the futility of non-co-operation, their leader himself openly defied the mandate of the Gauhati Congress to throw out the grants and reject the Finance Bill, thus driving the last nail into the coffin of obstruction. Like the Moderates of the first Assembly, the Swarajists rose to their responsibilities, consented to the grants, and passed the taxation proposals with only unimportant alterations. What the then President, Sir Frederick Whyte, described as a new note of persuasion and genuine advocacy in the argument of the Government Members which prevailed in the first Assembly was also discernible in the second and third Assembly on the Opposition benches. It is better to draw a veil over the intervening period of obstruction led by Mr Patel, which the Swarajists managed to survive by banishing him into the loneliness and silence of the Speaker's chair.

No one can lightly dispute the triumph of the reforms. Had the non-co-operators persisted in their boycott of the Legislatures, perhaps the atmosphere for constitutionalism would have been destroyed. The faith of the Moderates in the reforms and the determination of the Government to work the reforms notwithstanding all attempts to wreck them vanquished the extremists. The change of the storm-centre from the country outside to the Legislatures of the land sounded the death-knell of the Gandhi movement, and proclaimed the triumph of Montagu after his death.

The late Mr Montagu had many unkind critics, both among Europeans and Indians, in his lifetime, but his memory will be embalmed—as the great Brahmin of Bengal, Sir Surendranath, prophesied—in the affectionate recollections of unborn generations. Though the Liberals and Moderates as a party were defeated at the elections of 1923, Liberalism was accepted—after the customary explanations of hair-splitting politicians—as the Swarajist creed.

The triumph of the Liberals, however, was not easily achieved. They had to fight the scorn of public opinion, which steadily increased as the Ali brothers and Mr Gandhi urged the masses nearer to the brink of revolution. Month by month the position of the Members of the Legislative Assembly and the Provincial Councils became more and more difficult, for the wave of non-co-operation which was sweeping over India broke against those who co-operated in any way with the Government in public insult and social boycott and wild threats. The pages of Police Administration Reports for 1921 and 1922 bear testimony to the terrible situation against which the Liberals and their organs in the Press, the Government, and non-official Europeans fought. The fearful disaster of the Moplah rebellion, the revolutionary movement among the fighting Sikhs in the Punjab, the strenuous attempt to start mass civil disobedience in certain parts of Gujrat, the boycott of the Prince of Wales and the filling of the prisons by Nationalists and non-co-operators, were dread portents to the Moderates and Liberals, who honestly believed that they were supporting the Government against what the *Leader* newspaper of Allahabad described as "the criminal madness of non-co-operation."

So grim was the determination of the Liberals, Moderates, and Independents to break up the non-co-operation movement and support the Government in its resistance to it that a resolution which was moved by a Mohammedan Member at the beginning of 1922, to release from gaol the Ali brothers, the powerful leaders of the Khalifat movement, who were undergoing imprisonment, was not even seconded! When the resolution was put to the vote, after the Assembly had listened to the trenchant philippic from the Home Member, the mover himself retracted his support to it! The resolution was lost without one vote in its favour.

The great C. R. Das punished the Liberals for their co-operation with a foreign Government to crush the National movement. He drove them into the wilderness by capturing every Liberal seat in the elections of 1923. His less gifted successor quarrelled with his own colleagues, made the Liberal methods his own in 1926, and sought the Liberal support for lowering the Congress flag of independence in 1928.

To go back to 1921 and 1922, in every part of the province *jathas* of Sikhs armed with *kirpans* marched in military fashion to some shrine which they tried to take possession of. There were strikes of a political kind in different parts of India. The frontier was uneasy. The burden on the Indian Government was felt by their Liberal allies to be growing unbearable. The Assembly treated the non-co-operators as any Government would treat revolutionary agitators, no matter what their station in life. The moral backing of the classes which the Assembly represented, the most loyal and sober in the country, was wholly with the Government. Throughout the life of the first Assembly this relentless attitude was maintained toward political prisoners.

"I take the full share of my responsibility for the condemnation of Mr Gandhi," said Sir Tej Bahadur Sapru a year later to a representative of the *Review of Reviews*. The Moderates were giving proof of their fitness for responsible government by supporting the maintenance of law and order.

While thus prepared to support 'repression,' as their critics in the Congress described the Liberal policy, as early as the second session of the first Assembly, which began in September 1921, a resolution was moved relating to the grant of full autonomy in the provinces, the introduction of responsibility in the Central Government in 1923, and the grant of full Dominion status at the end of nine years. Nine years have since passed, and the Moderate demands have been embodied in a joint report of the Congress and the Liberal League under the flattering title "the Nehru Report," named after the discredited leader of the Congress Party!

Though no indication was given of the grant of full

Dominion status, the leader of the Congress Party declared from a score of platforms that he would be satisfied with Dominion status, even though it were not full. The Moderates did not really mean that they wanted full Dominion status in nine years, but only followed the Oriental way of bargaining which any Western tourist in an Indian bazaar must have noted as a peculiar Eastern characteristic. The European critic was amused in 1921 by the academic demand to pass an Act granting Dominion status at the end of nine years. He called it a child's sand-castle on the seashore.

If words were soldiers the Assembly might have won Dominion status in nine weeks. Its first speakers profusely quoted from tributes paid by high authorities to the ability and capacity of the Indian Legislature, not being sure of those qualities themselves. When the Swarajists entered the Legislatures they dispensed with the necessity of quoting alien authorities, but made the bold assertion of their unquestionable competence. Successive Home Members, Sir William Vincent, Sir Malcolm Hailey, the late Sir Alexander Muddiman, and Sir James Crerar, maintained, each in his own way, that there could be no long leaps to responsible government.

The Assembly of September 1921 abandoned its resolution for Dominion status in favour of a compromise between the Government and the Opposition, which recommended to "the Governor-General in Council that he should convey to the Secretary of State the view of this Assembly that the progress made by India on the path of responsible government warrants re-examination and revision of the present constitution at an earlier date than 1929." This view was accepted by Lord Birkenhead some years after, and a Reforms Commission was appointed before the expiry of the statutory period.

Among other things, an important resolution which was moved in the Delhi session of 1922 was for the association of standing committees with the various departments of the Government of India. The resolution was accepted by the Assembly, and the committees were accordingly brought into existence. Other resolutions of the same kind dealt with important matters, such as the modification of electoral rules, the functions of the Council of State, the Imperial Services, the appointment of Indians to secretariat appointments.

Resolutions adopted by the non-officials in the Legislature are not binding on the Government. The resolutions are only a means of bringing popular needs to the notice of the Government and influencing its policy in regard to them. How far the first Assembly succeeded by patient co-operation in influencing decisions and shaping the policy of the Government may be briefly surveyed.

On February 16, 1923, a Member of the Legislative Assembly moved the following resolution:

> This Assembly recommends to the Governor-General in Council that a policy of Protection be adopted as the one best suited to the interests of India, its application being regulated from time to time by such discrimination as may be considered necessary by the Government of India with the consent and approval of the Indian Legislature.

On behalf of the Government an amendment to this resolution was moved which suggested certain safeguards, but left the principle unchanged. This amendment was passed by the Assembly. Henceforth India's tariff policy became one of discriminating Protection.

In the same session another debate which took place showed something of the Legislature's influence in matters vitally affecting India's economic and industrial progress. The non-official demand was that the Governor-General in Council

> may be pleased to accept and give effect to the recommendation of the Chairman and four other members of the Indian

Railway Committee, 1920–21, that the undertakings of guaranteed Railway Companies, as and when the contracts fall in, should be entrusted to the direct management of the State.

The Government objected strongly to the extreme nature of the amendment, and pleaded that the door should not be closed against any well-considered scheme for company management.

The Assembly, however, carried an amendment in the following form:

> This Assembly recommends to the Governor-General in Council that he may be pleased, on expiry of their leases, to take over both the East Indian Railway and the Great Indian Peninsular Railway for management by the State.[1]

The Government have since given effect to the Assembly's decision. The East Indian Railway passed under State management in 1924, the Great Indian Peninsular Railway in 1925, and the Burma Railways in 1929.

Incidentally, the fact that the Government themselves have accepted the lead of the Assembly in the matter of State management shows that there was no justification for the observation that this essentially commercial undertaking was approached by the Indian representatives with "a certain political bias."[2]

Another way in which the Assembly influenced the decision of the Government is through the standing and other committees of the Central Legislature. Signs are not wanting that the committee system in India may develop on the lines of the American or the Continental rather than of the English system. The functions of the House of Commons committees are essentially different from those performed by the committees of the American

[1] *Proceedings* of the Delhi session of the Indian Legislative Assembly, 1923.

[2] *India in 1922–23*, by the Publicity Officer of the Government of India, p. 183.

Congress and the Continental Parliaments. Both Houses of the British Parliament consider the subjects which are brought before each of them when it sits as a 'House' and also 'in committee,' and thus the thorough discussion of the details of legislature and financial proposals is done by the whole House, instead of by committees chosen from among its members. Some in India may desire to adopt the English system, but it has led to so much congestion of business that Englishmen themselves are considering how best to revise it. A system of committees is now being experimented on, but the American system, whereby the committee can shape a Bill, and ask Ministers to appear before it to give their views, which may be ignored, is not likely to be copied in England. In India, however, something of the sort may be expected to develop.

A propos the committees, mention may be made of the Standing Finance Committee elected by the Assembly, and the Public Accounts Committee, on both of which the present writer has served. The former consists of not more than ten members, together with a member of the Assembly as Chairman, who is nominated by the Governor-General in Council, and the latter consists of not more than twelve members. They are elected at the beginning of each financial year. The Public Accounts Committee is formed in pursuance of a rule made under Section 67 of the 1919 Act. The Standing Finance Committee has no such statutory authority. Its formation was proposed by the Government and approved by the Assembly. It deals with proposals for expenditure before they come on to the Budget, with supplementary votes to meet unforeseen expenditure, and with large schemes for fresh expenditure which are put forward by the departments. Though technically the functions of the Committee are only advisory, the committee has already made its influence felt, as the following instance will show.

During the Delhi session of 1922, when the Finance

Member proposed the election of members of the Committee on Public Accounts, a private member moved that the functions of the Finance Committee should be so defined as to include the scrutiny of all proposals for new votable expenditure, the sanction of allotments out of lump-sum grants, and suggestions for retrenchments and economy in expenditure. The Finance Member accepted this suggestion.

The Standing Finance Committee is a departure from the English model. The Committee on Public Accounts corresponds to the Public Accounts Committee in England. Besides scrutinizing the accounts and calling the attention of the Assembly to any case in which there has been a waste of public money or an offence against financial rules, the Public Accounts Committee has certain constructive powers, and can compare the expenditure of one department with that of another, and point out the possibilities of exercising economies in various ways. The influence exercised by the Public Accounts Committee is evidenced by the fact that some of its suggestions have led to certain changes in the form of demands for grants. Territorial grants have been arranged on a more logical basis, and large items, such as the expenditure on Currency Stores, have been removed from the grant of the High Commissioner for India.

Testimony to the non-official members' appreciation of the utility of the committees was furnished when a private member moved a resolution in the Delhi session of 1922 proposing the association of the Standing Committees with the various departments of the Government of India, which was adopted and subsequently given effect to. Panels were elected by the Assembly, from which the members of the committees were chosen. The Railway Advisory Committee, which, it is the general complaint, does not meet often enough, paved the way for a change of vast administrative importance made by the second Assembly in September 1924 by separating railway finance from general finance. Though the present power of control of the Central and Local Advisory Committee of the railways is not sufficient, it is certain that as years roll by the administration of the railways will be more closely examined by these committees, whose influence is bound to grow.

Another aspect under which the subject may be dealt with is the appointment of the Joint Committees of the Legislative Assembly and the Council of State from time to time for certain purposes. In England Joint Committees of Parliament are not unknown. The Government of India Bill, for instance, was referred to a Parliamentary Joint Committee. Such first-class matters apart, the Joint Committees of the British Parliament generally deal with private Bills, which have no counterpart in India, or with the rules regulating the communications between the Lords and the Commons. The Joint Committee of the Central Legislature, however, besides dealing with important matters, such as the examination of the possibilities of financial retrenchment, also report on a Bill relating to intestate and testamentary succession. They were also, until lately, associated with the British Parliamentary Commission in a task of momentous importance, like the examination of the question of constitutional reforms.

The growth of the committee system is not regulated by any provisions of the Act. It shows how the constitution has in it certain inherent powers which must grow as they have grown in England, with the very working of the constitution itself.

One of the important battles of the Assembly has been fought on the question of financial control. It is natural that Indian representatives should devote considerable attention to this. Students of English and American history are aware of the great part played by the people in their fight for financial control.

The provisions of the 1919 Act are not generous in regard to the question of popular control of the finances of the country. Important items of expenditure have, in fact, been removed from the control of the Assembly. But the non-officials have missed no opportunity of voicing their protest against this and several other similar restrictions. Particularly, the lack of control over the Military Budget, the larger part of which is non-votable, has been the subject of constant criticism during the Budget discussions. Thus has public opinion been brought powerfully to bear on these sacrosanct items.

One important fact must be set down in passing. The Standing Finance Committee is serving the purpose of establishing intimate contact between the Government and the Opposition. It is worthy of note that the Swarajists who entered the Councils with the cry of 'boycott' are clamouring for places to-day in these committees. Scenes have taken place at their party meetings in the general scramble for support of the individual Swarajists aspiring for places in the Standing Committees. This is a significant omen. Constitutionalism has vanquished obstruction!

As a further proof of the triumph of constitutionalism may be mentioned the interesting fact that even the Swarajist members of the Standing Finance Committee have realized their responsibility and spoken on the floor of the House in defence of the Government on items over which controversies have arisen. This is indeed a link in the golden chain that binds the powers that be and the Opposition—a chain not forged so much by the Reforms Act as by the new spirit of developing its growth by creating helpful precedents in an atmosphere of harmony.

Well might those who respect Mr Montagu's memory claim that the reforms have grown and expanded beyond the actual framework as desired by him, showing thereby that his constitution has not only survived the violent assaults made on it, but is living and growing. The superficial observer sees this not. Young men in a hurry miss the roots that are striking deep into the soil. Old men are impatient to gather the fruits within their lifetime.

The interest taken in the Legislature by its members was intense. In the first Assembly a hundred Bills were introduced, sixty-three by private members. Of the Government Bills sixty were passed, one was 'certified,' one was rejected by the Assembly, and one was withdrawn by the Government after introduction. Two were circulated for public consideration, and one was referred to a Select Committee. Of the private members' Bills, nine were passed, eight rejected, and one disallowed. The others were circulated for public consideration or referred to select committees. One was passed by the Assembly, but rejected by the Council of State. These measures were of wide and varied interest, embracing as they did industrial, agricultural, commercial, social, political, legal, educational, and other subjects.

There was no dearth of industrial legislation aiming at improvements in the conditions of factory life. For instance, the Workmen's Compensation Act, providing for compensation in case of accidents involving death or total or partial disablement; the Indian Electricity Amendment Act, securing uniformity of rules in regard to hydro-electric schemes in the different provinces; the Labour Disputes Bill, aiming at the cessation of the exploitation of labour for political purposes and the settlement of purely industrial disputes between labour and capital; social legislation, raising the age of consent; the North-West Provinces Inquiry; the inquiry into the necessity for the establishment of a military college by a mixed committee of officials and non-officials, known as the Skeen Committee, named after the President, Sir Andrew Skeen; the Repeal of the Press Act; and, last but not least, the appointment of a Labour Commission to inquire into and report on the condition of labour and make recommendations for its amelioration are some of the achievements of the Legislative Assembly.

Among other achievements of the Assembly must be mentioned the Racial Distinctions Bill. It did not arouse the angry passions of an earlier day in which the Ilbert Bill, notwithstanding the Viceroy's enthusiasm, floundered. The passage of the Racial Distinctions Bill through the Assembly met with the natural opposition of the European Members, which, however, ceased with the Assembly's assent to it. This shows that a new spirit of democracy has come to stay in the land—a spirit which is respected by Europeans and Indians alike. An official report says:

> The passage of the Racial Distinctions Bill, introduced as a result of the appointment of a committee to investigate the differences in the criminal trials of Indian and European subjects of the King, marked an important stage in the attainment of equality between the two races in India.[1]

The work of the Assembly and the vast amount of non-official interpellations, resolutions, and Bills disclose the hunger for constructive legislation in our erstwhile destructive critics.

A study of the resolutions and activities of the second and third Assemblies will show how the Legislatures have exercised a sobering influence on the ardent spirits. The Congress had boycotted, as we have seen, the first Assembly and the other Legislatures of the land. The Congress did not formally sanction that its organizations should take active part in supporting the Swarajists against the non-Congress parties in the elections of 1923. In 1926 we find the Congress becoming an election caucus. The successful campaign of the Madras leader, Mr S. Srinivasa Iyengar, was recognized by his election as the President of the Congress for the year 1926–27. We find, further, that the leader of the Swaraj Party in the Assembly was elected as

[1] *India in 1922–23*, p. 99.

the President of the National Congress for the year 1928–29. The name of the Swaraj Party itself was changed into the "Congress Party." Its programme of obstruction and non-co-operation was altogether abandoned. What was once the "National" Congress became an electioneering organization for purposes of party. One of its stormy petrels has been working the reforms for all they are worth with the sanction of his party in his capacity as the President of the Legislative Assembly.

CHAPTER IV

SIMLA—AND WHITEHALL

In one of his fascinating utterances Lord Birkenhead compared the educated Indians to Englishmen, and expressed the conviction that they aspired with the rest of the English-speaking world for democratic institutions which had developed in England through successive centuries. According to Tacitus, the Germanic forest tribes who were the ancestors of the Englishmen of to-day had instinct in them the principles of democracy. The British constitution is an embodiment of those principles. England attained democracy by the manifestation of its Anglo-Saxon soul. The national character of England is writ large on the English constitution. Common sympathies, willing union of different peoples, a readiness to co-operate among themselves, says John Stuart Mill, go to constitute a nationality. These virtues have moulded into one nation the Scotsmen, the Welshmen, and the Englishmen who make modern Britain and bring glory to her name. Unless those virtues are assimilated by the peoples of India the development of a homogeneous national will to action—which is the only guarantee of stable nationalism—is inconceivable.

The problem of national unity has not yet been solved in India, though repeated attempts have been made to solve it. All honour to those who have made them; but their repeated failure reveals how the Queen-mother India cannot yet wear the crown and symbol of her nationhood. The disruptive forces are still there, and until they are brought under control nationalism must abdicate. It is this fear that stipulated that the development of the Indian democracy shall be by stages. Judging from the omens, the cautious formula of autonomy in driblets will be abandoned in the provinces, but adhered to more rigidly than ever in the sphere of the Central Government.

It is stated that the problem of every province in India repeats in miniature the problem of India herself. When the provinces in their own limited sphere are endowed with provincial Dominion status that will make the attainment of National Home Rule easy.

Under the present constitution the Government of India and the Provincial Governments are responsible to the Secretary of State for India. Technically, therefore, Whitehall is omnipotent.

According to a section of the 1919 Act, the Secretary of State may "superintend, direct, and control all acts, operations, and concerns which relate to the Government or revenues of India, etc." But a subsection which follows shows that some change has come over the position of the Secretary of State, that it is not the same *vis-à-vis* the Government of India. Under this subsection the old practice has been stopped of paying the salary of the Secretary of State from the revenues of India.

In their report on the Government of India Bill, 1919, the Joint Select Committee of Parliament laid down that in the relations of the Secretary of State with the Governor-General in Council the Committee were of opinion that no statutory change could be made so long as the Governor-General remained responsible to Parliament; but in practice the conventions which governed the relations might wisely be modified to meet fresh circumstances caused by the creation of a Legislative Assembly with a large elected majority. It was further laid down that in the exercise of his responsibility to Parliament the Secretary of State might reasonably consider that only in exceptional circumstances should he be called upon to intervene in matters of purely Indian interest, where the Government and the Legislature of India were in agreement.

The rules made under the Act restrict the intervention of the Secretary of State in regard to "Transferred subjects," which are under the control of the Ministers, who are responsible to the Legislatures, save in regard to inter-provincial matters affecting Imperial interests, such as provincial loans, to which the Secretary of State or the High Commissioner for India is a party. The restriction of the intervention of the Secretary of State was not relished by some prominent Conservatives. The following episode in Parliament is *à propos*:

VISCOUNT CURZON. I desire to ask you, sir, a question with regard to the ruling given yesterday on a question in reference to India. I asked a question with reference to a certain man in India. . . .

You replied that it did not seem to be a matter for Parliament, but one for the Legislative Council. The Honourable Member for South Kensington then asked, " Is it not a matter for this House to know whether a man who has been appointed to high office under the Crown is a convicted rebel ? "

MR SPEAKER. The House, having practically given Home Rule, or something in the nature of Home Rule, to these Councils, the less it interferes with these Councils the better.

VISCOUNT CURZON. When a country has been given Home Rule, are we to understand that no further questions may be asked about the details of administration in that country ?

MR SPEAKER. We are now commencing a new era in India, and it appears to me that it would be extremely undesirable if this House were to attempt to undertake the function of controlling or criticizing the Ministers who are responsible to the newly created legislative bodies. After all, the Ministers, however chosen, are the Ministers of those legislative bodies, they presumably have their confidence, their salaries are voted by them. I think that we had far better begin by abstaining from asking questions and criticizing the Ministers who have been duly selected by the Governor, under the statutory powers which this House has given him for that purpose.[1]

[1] Hansard for February 24, 1921, p. 1148.

The Speaker's ruling reveals that the spirit of the recommendations of the Joint Committee of Parliament in regard to the Indian reforms has found general acceptance in the British Parliament.

Another instance is the weakening of the Secretary of State's control over Indian Legislation. Under the Morley-Minto reforms the Secretary of State required prior report of all the principal Bills of the Government of India, not those of a formal nature. The Secretary of State virtually dictated to the Government of India the abandonment or modification of such Bills. The prior report practice still continues, but only of Bills affecting the discipline or maintenance of his Majesty's military, naval, or air forces, and the public debt or customs duties. Even in regard to these Bills his intervention is practically restricted to making suggestions.

With the appointment of a High Commissioner for India in London (1920) all the agency functions which the Secretary of State used to perform have been transferred to the High Commissioner. With the advance of India to Dominion status the power of the High Commissioner will increase, and that of the Secretary of State correspondingly decrease.

Though the provisions of the 1919 Act seem drastic—they certainly are drastic in some respects, and Indian opinion will not be wholly satisfied until the Secretary of State for India is reduced to the position of the Colonial Secretary—nevertheless the relations of the Secretary of State with the Government of India have become less rigid and more plastic. Viceroys like Lord Curzon and Lord Minto have placed on record the nature of the interference of the Secretary of State, who could not have such a real grasp of the situation as the man on the spot. Contrasting the powers that used to be exercised by the Secretary of State with the relaxed control which he has at present, official opinion is apt to think that the change is so vast and so considerable that it almost amounts to a revolution. Indian opinion, however, considers the change too tardy and unsatisfactory.

The policy underlying the reforms is naturally cautious. It was agreed among all conservative statesmen in England that in the first place India must make an immediate start on her road to responsible government, and, secondly, full self-government, or Dominion status, was the ultimate goal which only an India united in the fullest sense of the term could attain. The reformed constitution, where it deals with the provincial government, is a bold compromise between autocracy and democracy. Where it deals with the Central Government, however, it is a curious admixture of the forms of democracy with the reality of autocracy. The democratic form is in the non-official majority. The autocracy is naked in the fact that the Government of India's power is undiminished for dealing with external invasion and internal commotion. The Simon Commission may say that the reforms do not contemplate the immediate diminution of the Central Government's power in regard, especially, to its responsibility for the safety of India's people. This position was never accepted by the Indian public as a whole; those with a liberal outlook co-operated and hoped for better things through co-operation. The larger section of non-co-operators resorted to resistance.

The position of the Governor-General has not been impaired by the reforms. With his Executive Council he is the supreme monarch of all he surveys. In certain respects he is more powerful than his Council.

In the Morley-Minto times there were six members, one of whom was an Indian, in the Governor-General's Executive Council. Under the Montagu dispensation this racial restriction was done away with. Three of the members must be public servants of at least ten years' standing is the only stipulation. This is deliberate and of far-reaching consequence, because there is no limit now to the number of Indians who may be members of the Council. A convention has been established that at least three of the members of the Council should be Indians out of the six ordinary members.

The Law Members of the Viceroy's Executive Council need not now have English or Scottish qualifications, but may be pleaders of ten years' standing of an Indian High Court. For instance, Sir Tej Bahadur Sapru, a former Law Member of the Government of India, had no English or Scottish qualifications. He was an advocate of the Allahabad High Court.

This broadening of the foundation, as it were, of the Governor-General's Executive Council has introduced a process which, as recorded in the Parliamentary Joint Select Committee's report, has large possibilities: "The members of the Council drawn from the ranks of the public servants will, as time goes on, be more and more likely to be of Indian rather than of European extraction."

The Governor-General and not India's Parliament is wholly responsible for the safety, tranquillity, or interest of British India. If a prophecy may be risked, the Simon Commission do not contemplate an early transference of this responsibility. The members of the Opposition in India's Parliament have adversely commented on the power of "certification," according to which, if the Governor-General believes that some particular measure is essential to the safety and interests of British India, he can pass it into law in the teeth of the Legislature's opposition and rejection.

On the financial side the Legislature has no statutory power over supplies for the Army, the public debt, etc. Its power is restricted either to vote or to refuse a large range of supplies. Even this restricted power is nullified by the power of appropriation with which the Governor-General is invested. If any particular item is refused the

Governor-General or the Governor-General in Council can appropriate it if he thinks it sufficiently important to warrant his doing so.

Powers similar to these, says the official apologist, have been exercised by the President of the United States. The President is an elected autocrat, but the Viceroy is the symbol of alien supremacy, retorts the Indian Nationalist.

When the Indian States (Protection against Disaffection) Bill was introduced during the Simla Session of the Assembly in 1922 it was opposed by a majority. The repeal of the Press Laws in British India resulted in a demand for protection from the Princes. Their administration is more vigorously criticized by newspapers printed in British India, which have more liberty, than by newspapers in the States, if there are newspapers at all there. The Princes do not believe in a free Press in their own territories. It must also be admitted that some of the vernacular newspapers who specially devote themselves to this anti-Princes propaganda are venomous blackmailers with no democratic aspirations. Be that as it may, the Legislative Assembly would not give permission to introduce the Bill. Some of its members were carried away by ideas of a free Press and liberty of criticism. Others felt that constant exposure of the maladministration and cruelty in Indian States was the only check on the autocracy of the Princes.

The Government, however, following the terms of ambiguous treaties, and in accordance with equivocal pronouncements in the past regarding the status of Princes and Chiefs, stood by the Princes. The Governor-General decided to "certify" the Princes Protection Bill, which accordingly became law.

Again, in face of non-official opposition, the Governor-General certified the restoration of the salt tax in the Delhi Session of 1923. The salt tax is the most unpopular form of taxation. The maintenance of an increased tax on salt was imprudent. Bureaucratic statesmanship, which was bankrupt in Simla-Delhi, instead of resorting to other avenues, insisted on defying public opinion. In justification of their action the Government pointed to the importance of a balanced Budget, and pretended that they knew no other way of balancing the Budget. There could be no two opinions that a balanced Budget was of the utmost consequence in a country like India, but the non-official object was directed against the method adopted. The official view was that the incidence of the salt tax itself of a few annas per head per annum would be hardly perceptible. This view was endorsed by the Council of State. Thus fortified, the Governor-General certified the tax after its reasoned rejection by the Legislative Assembly. If the Government had a General Election to face, as in England, they would not have increased the salt tax to balance the Budget, or, having increased it, would have been swept into the wilderness.

It is customary for official writers to compare this power of the Viceroy of certification to the Imperial veto on colonial legislation. Say the politicians, India too will not object to a similar Imperial veto, which is seldom exercised, when endowed with colonial autonomy. The official reply to this is, when a section of the extremists have as their party-cry obstruction with a view to make rule by certification normal, the politician has himself to blame. The power to veto, we are told, in the United States' President is real and frequently used. Mr Cleveland, during his eight years as President of the United States, employed it on more than three hundred occasions. But America has self-government. More correctly, the Indian constitution is like that of the Philippines. The Reforms Act of 1919 is like the Jones Law of 1916, which was "an Act to declare the purpose of the people of the United States as to the future political status of the people of the Philippine Islands, and to provide a more autonomous Government for those islands."

The Jones Law was in one respect different from the Indian Act—it did not give the Governor-General of the Philippines statutory powers of certification in case of a disagreement with the Legislature. The British Government obviously profited by the American omission, to repair which the Woods-Forbes Commission went out to the Philippines in 1921. It is always disastrous to go back on reforms. What is given cannot be taken away. An excess of caution in the beginning, followed by a gradual progress in recklessness, is the way of statesmanship!

The Governor-General's powers of veto and certification were not pleasing to the Nationalists in the Legislatures. The Congress Party in the Assembly made a point of forcing the Governor-General to use his extraordinary powers as often as possible. They played this trick especially by moving the omission of some Budget demands, which, with the help of other parties, they carried. Their endeavour, however, to throw out the Finance Bill was repeatedly frustrated by the other parties refusing to go the whole hog in obstruction. Consequently, the Congress Party vented its childish wrath upon the Governor-General personally by peevishly boycotting the Viceregal functions in the Viceroy's house, even though its crazy leader never missed a single opportunity to establish contact with the Governor-General at social functions given in the house of the Speaker. This stupid inconsistency only shows that the Swarajist leadership under Nehru is as mad as a March hare.

CHAPTER V

THE CONGRESS MOVEMENT

THE Congress of to-day has undergone fundamental changes in programme, policy, and outlook far beyond the dream of its originators. The present leaders of the Congress and its rank and file have not that remarkable faith in British justice and fair play which inspired its early founders. Incredible is the change that has come over the Congress within the last forty years. The Congress has moved ahead of the times. To-day it performs not its old function of mirroring the minds of the majority of the sober people of India, but of leading the combustible masses to aggressive political action.

The first impetus to Indian nationalism came from Edmund Burke's impeachment of Warren Hastings, Macaulay's attack on British rule in India, and Bright's downright speeches in Parliament. "Thirty millions of human beings," wrote Macaulay,

> were reduced to an extremity of wretchedness. They had been accustomed to live under tyranny, but never under tyranny like this. That Government, oppressive as the most oppressive form of barbarian despotism, was strong with all the strength of civilization.

Such fierce criticisms by frank Englishmen who were dissatisfied with the imperfections of early British administration—imperfections inevitable at the outset of any foreign rule—hastened the rapid evolution of some ordinary and ordered government. The Indian Civil Service, European in character and constitution, was established ; a judicial system was adopted ; and the administration of the Land Revenue was taken up.

Queen Victoria issued her famous proclamation of 1858, promising equal opportunities for all, irrespective of race and creed, declaring that "in their prosperity will be our strength, in their contentment our security, and in their gratitude our reward."

Bright said :

> All over those vast regions there are countless millions helpless and defenceless, deprived of their natural leaders and their ancient chiefs, looking with only some small ray of hope to that omnipresent and irres.stible power by which they have been subjected. . . .
>
> Is it possible to touch a chord in the heart of Englishmen to raise them to a sense of the miseries inflicted on that unhappy country by crimes and blunders of our rulers here ? If you have steeled your hearts against the natives, if nothing can stir you to sympathy with their miseries, at least have pity upon your own countrymen.

If the general administration was far from satisfactory, the financial mismanagement was even worse. Henry Fawcett characterized it as "magnificent meanness." The British Government concluded that matters had reached the stage when an inquiry should be undertaken. A Parliamentary Committee was appointed with Fawcett himself as its Chairman to inquire into the financial administration of India. Fawcett's inquiry brought him into close touch with Indians, for whose welfare he always strove hard in Parliament, but it could not stop that financial extravagance inevitably associated with every foreign rule. Fawcett was defeated in one of the General Elections. English-educated Indians, who were the only politically minded people at the time, raised a subscription of £750 to enable him to get into Parliament at the next earliest possible opportunity, which he did, to serve India with redoubled earnestness.

Neither the "Indian member," as Fawcett came to be

called, nor other friends of India were satisfied with the impression they could produce on Parliament. Fawcett felt that what Macaulay had said of Parliamentary indifference to India in the Company days was no less true under the Crown:

> A broken head on Cold-Bath fields produces a greater sensation amongst us than three pitched battles in India. A few weeks ago we had to decide on a claim brought by an individual against the revenues of India. If it had been an English question the walls would scarcely have held the members who would have flocked to the division. It was an Indian question; and we could scarcely, by dint of application, make a house. Even when my right honourable friend, the President of the Board of Control, gave his able and interesting explanation of the plan which he intended to propose for the Government of a hundred million human beings, the attendance was not so large as I have often seen it on a turnpike Bill or railroad Bill.

Disraeli's Government appointed Lord Lytton as the Viceroy, and he, instead of taking up the work of popular welfare, addressed himself to the costly task of raising "a scientific frontier," besides conducting expensive expeditions against Afghanistan to the detriment of the taxpayer. Lord Lytton's policy was called into question by the public, especially in the vernacular Press, which was freely expressing the considered opinion of the country, unsavoury to the autocracy. Lord Lytton would neither face his critics nor look into their grievances. He ventured on a new law, whereby he could gag the expression of uncomfortable opinion—a method which his successors have from time to time faithfully copied when placed in similar predicaments.

In spite of the Vernacular Press Act, the heroic band of early workers continued undaunted. The *Amrita Bazar Patrika* of Bengal was dramatically converted in one night into an English newspaper. Other papers in the English language sprang into existence. A vigorous agitation was started. Meetings were held in the principal towns of India. Babu (later Sir) Surendranath Bannerjee, who had entered politics after dismissal from the Indian Civil Service, toured the country, rousing the people to a sense of their duties and responsibilities.

The increasing disturbance in the mind of the educated classes did not seem to have passed unnoticed, when a wise, able, and sympathetic statesman in the person of Lord Ripon was appointed as the Viceroy of India. Soon after his assumption of the reins of administration Lord Ripon carried out salutary measures of reform. He repealed the Vernacular Press Act. He inaugurated the beginnings of local self-government, which he considered as the foundation of national self-government.

Lord Ripon did not impart any original conception of local self-government into his scheme. He had the imagination to realize that the reorganization of village *panchayats*, which had stood the test of ages, on modern lines would greatly conduce to the benefit of the country. Municipal bodies in large areas were no doubt unified and organized by them with a view to facilitating the work of the District Magistrate and Collector, but, as an English writer put it, "two hundred and odd district councils and the seven hundred municipalities of British India have, compared with the ancient institutions of the village, a somewhat artificial air."

Lord Ripon's successors did not share his enthusiasm. The opposition of the Indian Civil Service and non-official Europeans to Lord Ripon's reforming zeal reached its climax when he introduced the famous Ilbert Bill (1883) with the object of removing the ban on the Indian Magistracy in regard to the trial of European offenders. The Viceroy was reviled in the Anglo-Indian Press with a ferocity unknown to Indian journalism before. The character and competence of the people of India, too, were attacked by the leaders of an "Anglo-Indian Defence Association," which was formed to conduct an offensive campaign against Lord Ripon and the Ilbert Bill. Not satisfied with constitutional agitation and un-Parliamentary language, the Anglo-Indian extremists went a step farther. They wanted to try conclusions with a Viceroy who had the temerity to introduce reforms against the wish of the Anglo-Indian community. "A conspiracy had been formed," says Buckland,

> by a number of men in Calcutta, who had bound themselves in the event of Government adhering to their projected legislation to overpower the sentries at the Government House, to put the Viceroy on board a steamer at Chand Lal Ghat and send him to England *via* the Cape.[1]

Lord Ripon had to abandon at last a far-reaching scheme of fundamental principle and barest justice.

The Ilbert Bill controversy served as an eye-opener to the English-educated classes, who realized the value of organization in public life in bringing pressure to bear on the powers that be. It was also felt that if the Indian public were alert and disciplined the hands of a sympathetic Viceroy could be considerably strengthened and Anglo-Indian hostility effectively neutralized. The Indian Association of Calcutta organized a National Conference, with a view to starting what they described as "a constitutional agitation" for the rights and privileges of Indians. A new association called the National League was established in Bengal in 1884 to further safeguard the rights of the people. The Madras Mahajana Sabha was ushered into existence to awaken in the people of that Presidency a sense of national consciousness. The Presidency Association of Bombay and the Sarvajanik Sabha of Poona were doing useful service in their respective spheres.

The activities of the provincial organizations had to be guided by a national organization, the need for which

[1] See also *British Government in India*, by Lord Curzon, vol. ii, p. 243.

had dawned on the minds of the leaders of the time. Allan Octavian Hume, I.C.S., mentioned the idea to the then Viceroy, Lord Dufferin, who welcomed it. In the words of the late W. C. Bannerjee, a famous Calcutta barrister, whom Mr Hume had taken into his confidence, Lord Dufferin said that

> there was no body of persons in this country who performed the functions which her Majesty's Opposition did in England. The newspapers, even if they really represented the views of the people, were not reliable, and as the English were necessarily ignorant of what was thought of them and their policy, in the interests as well of the rulers as of the ruled Indian politicians should meet early and point out to the Government in what respects the administration was defective and how it could be improved.

When the first Congress met in Bombay in 1885 it pointed out to the Government its defects and shortcomings, and the ways and means of effecting an improvement. It demanded (*a*) the abolition of the Council of the Secretary of State; (*b*) the reform and expansion of the supreme and existing Local Legislative Councils; (*c*) the holding of simultaneous competitive examinations in England and in India for appointment in various civil departments of the Public Service, instead of in England only, as hitherto; (*d*) the reduction of the military expenditure.

The second session of the Congress, which was held at Calcutta in 1886, gave a definite shape to the reform proposals by formulating a tentative scheme according to which not less than one-half of the members of the enlarged Councils were to be elected, and not more than one-fourth to be officials. All legislative measures and financial questions, including Budgets, whether these involved net or enhanced taxation or not, were to be submitted to and dealt with by these Councils. The Congress scheme at the same time conceded to the Executive Government the power of overruling the decision of the majority of the Council in case the acceptance of that decision should be prejudicial to public interest. But it stipulated that the exercise of that power should be followed by the publication of the Government's explanation. If that failed to carry conviction the overruled majority could appeal to the Standing Committee, which, if necessary, could report to the full House.

The Congress also asked for the extension of the system of trial by jury to many parts of the country where it was not in existence; the withdrawal of the power vested in Sessions Judges and High Courts of setting aside verdicts of acquittal, thus depriving the verdicts of juries of all finality; the introduction into the Indian Code of Criminal Procedure a provision similar to that embodied in the Summary Jurisdiction Act of England, enabling accused persons in warrant cases to demand, if they so desired, trial by the Court of Sessions, instead of by the Magistrate; and, last but not least, the complete separation of judicial and executive functions. The Calcutta Congress also appealed to the Government to authorize a system of volunteering.

The third session of the Congress, which was held at Madras, besides confirming the resolution of its predecessors, resolved (*a*) that the military service in its higher grades should be opened to Indians, and that military colleges should be established in India to educate and train Indians for a military career as officers of the Indian Army; (*b*) that the Arms Act be modified; (*c*) that a system of technical education be introduced to encourage indigenous manufactures and utilize indigenous talents and skill.

The demands of the Congress took Lord Dufferin aback. Speaking at the St Andrew's dinner at Calcutta on November 30, 1888, Lord Dufferin ridiculed the Congressmen as "a microscopic minority"—a phrase which has since become classical—and characterized their aim as "a big jump into the unknown."

When the fourth Congress met at Allahabad on

December 26 Mr George Yule, who presided, replied to the Viceroy's attack on the Congress. "Every great movement," said Yule, "has to pass through three stages, ridicule, abuse, and concession."

Charles Bradlaugh took up the cudgels against the Viceroy in England. Lord Dufferin felt the force of criticism, and was anxious not to be misunderstood. He explained in a letter which he wrote to Bradlaugh that he had not misrepresented the Congress; that he had neither directly nor by implication suggested that the Congress was seditious; that he always spoke of the Congress in terms of sympathy and respect, and treated its members with great personal civility; that he was always in favour of a Civil Service reform so that Indians might obtain more appointments in it, as proved by his appointment of the Indian Civil Service Commission; and that he himself was in favour of such a reform of the Provincial Councils as Bradlaugh appeared to advocate.

Lord Dufferin initiated discussions on the question of Council reforms, and his Committee recommended that Councils should see all papers freely, and discuss all matters openly, and that the Budget estimates should be considered by a Standing Committee and, if necessary, by the Councils themselves. The Dufferin Committee further suggested that not more than two-fifths of the members should be elected, and power should be reserved to Government to pass certain measures, even if the majority went against them.

Lord Dufferin himself was not prepared to go so far as his Committee. He said:

> No matter to what degree the liberalization of the Councils may take place, it will be necessary to leave in the hands of each Provincial Government the ultimate decision upon all important questions and the paramount control of its own policy. It is in this view that we have arranged that the nominated members of the Council should outnumber the elected members, at the same time that the Governor has been

empowered to overrule his Council whenever he feels himself called upon by circumstances to do so.

The Viceroy whittled away some of the radical proposals of his Committee. The Secretary of State turned down the Viceroy's recommendations. Lord Cross considered it "unwise" to introduce the principle of election, which, he said, was "a fundamental change." Mr Gladstone himself, speaking for the Opposition in the House of Commons, was not at all disposed to ask them at once to produce what he felt to be "large and imposing results," and would content himself by looking presumptively, with the greatest amount of expectation and hope, to the municipal bodies and the local authorities in India in which the elective element was already included.

The ninth Congress, which met at Lahore in 1893, resolved that in regard to the Council's Act of 1892 there should be material alterations alike in the rules of the Government of India and in the practice of most of the Local Governments, and further deplored that the Punjab should still be denied the right to be represented either in the Viceroy's or in any local council. Four years later the Punjab was given "the boon"—as the Congress in its exuberance of gratitude called it—of a Legislative Council, but the Councillors had neither the right of interpellation nor the people the right of recommending Councillors for nomination, which the other provinces enjoyed.

When the thirteenth Congress met at Amroati in 1897 it had to pronounce its verdict on a strange situation. The measures taken by the Government to deal with the first great outbreak of the bubonic plague in India shocked orthodoxy. The late Sir Valentine Chirol wrote:

> In such visitations the panic-stricken masses see, as they did in Europe in the Dark Ages, a manifestation of divine wrath which has to be submissively endured or appeased by prayers and incantations.

The British authorities, taken unawares by the suddenness and the violence of the epidemic, tried to stamp it out by drastic measures, sometimes not very wise or very wisely carried out, such as house-to-house visitations and segregation camps, more terrifying to the ignorant populace than the plague itself.

This was, in Chirol's words,

> an oppressive invasion of the Hindu home, outraging the sanctity of its domestic shrines and the modesty of its sheltered women. A murder followed. On June 27, 1897, the day of Queen Victoria's Diamond Jubilee, Mr Rand, a member of the Indian Civil Service, who was marked down as President of the Poona Plague Committee, was shot dead, together with Lieutenant Ayerst of the Commissariat Department, on the way back from the evening reception at Government House, by Damodhar Chapekar.

Chapekar was hanged. Mr Tilak and the editors of the two vernacular papers were prosecuted and sentenced; the Natu brothers, who had passionately appealed to the Government to interfere, were imprisoned without trial; and the British and the Anglo-Indian Press demanded that the vernacular paper should be gagged.

Lord George Hamilton, the Secretary of State for India, exclaimed in the House of Commons:

> In India, almost without warning, an apparently peaceful population might suddenly become as dangerous as criminal lunatics, with but one object before them—to murder the class alien to them.

Changes were proposed in the law of sedition which the Congressmen described as calculated to deal a severe blow to the liberty of speech and writing and to increase the powers of the police. The exercise of the special powers given by the Bengal Regulation III of 1818 and the Madras Regulation II of 1819 reminded the Congress of the *lettres de cachet* of Bourbon times. The quartering of the Punitive Police at Poona was disapproved.

The late Surendranath Bannerjee, the Demosthenes of India, addressed his people from the Congress platform:

> Brother delegates, security of life and property are the great foundations upon which rests the vast, the stupendous, the colossal fabric of British rule in India. What becomes of these inestimable blessings if at any moment your property may be confiscated, and you may be arrested and left in custody without a trial and without a word of explanation? What becomes of the boasted vaunt of the boon of personal liberty and personal security under British Rule under these circumstances?

The faith of the stalwarts of the Congress in British justice was so great, indeed, that Mr W. C. Bannerjee considered that the remedy to the situation lay in appealing to the British public. "I have no doubt," said he, "that the British Nation will rise in their wrath and free us from the trammels which Lord Elgin and his counsellors are forging for us."

The Congress passed the following resolutions:

> Resolved, that this Congress views with alarm and anxiety the changes proposed in the existing law of sedition, as defined in Section 124A, and of circulating false reports, as defined in Section 505 of the Indian Penal Code, and is of opinion that Section 124A of the Indian Penal Code requires amendment not in the direction of greater stringency, but in that of greater freedom, and if the law of sedition in India is to be made the same as it is in England, the administration of it should be safeguarded in substantially the same way as it is there—viz., that the trial of the accused persons must always be by jury, at least one-half of whom should be persons of the same nationality as the accused, and that their verdict should be unanimous. And this Congress strongly protests against cases of sedition being made by Magistrates and not by Courts of Sessions and High Courts exclusively, as hithertofore, and against the proposal to invest District Magistrates with the

power of calling upon persons who in their opinion disseminate disaffection, to find sureties of good behaviour for twelve months. This Congress is further of opinion that the changes in the law now proposed will be altogether at variance with the pledges given by Sir James FitzJames Stephen when passing Section 124A of the Indian Penal Code through the Council, and will deal an irreparable blow to liberty of speech and freedom of the Press, thus retarding the progress of the country and creating terror instead of confidence in the minds of the people.

Resolved, that this Congress desires to record its protest against the Criminal Procedure Bill of 1897, now pending before the Imperial Legislative Council, as being a retrograde and reactionary measure which will add to the already large powers of the police, invest Magistrates with a discretionary authority which they do not now possess, and curtail the powers of the High Courts, all to the extreme prejudice of accused persons.[1]

The Congressmen grumbled that the demands of the Indian National Congress did not receive prompt consideration. It was time that some concessions were made. The Congress complained year after year that its resolutions on matters administrative, military, financial, and legal were ignored by a deaf Government.

Between 1880 and 1900 there were four famines. The Congress gravely opined that these famines were due to the appalling poverty, intensified by the enormous drain of the national wealth, excessive taxation, and over-assessment brought on by a policy of waste adopted by the Government both in the civil and military departments. The elders of the Congress waited in deputation on the Viceroy, and sent their representatives to England.

The first delegation came to England in 1889; a year after another influential delegation followed. Mr W. C. Bannerjee and Dadabhai Naoroji practically made England their second home, and the latter entered Parliament in

[1] *The Indian National Congress Report.*

course of time. An influential British Congress Committee was appointed, and the Congress voted Rs. 45,000 for its expenses. In 1890 the weekly *India* was started under the editorship of Mr William Digby, who wrote a book in which he attacked the Indian administration from a financial and economic standpoint. An Indian Parliamentary Committee was organized with a view to enlightening the Members of Parliament on Indian affairs.

Congress propaganda in England, and especially in the lobbies of Parliament, resulted in the appointment of a Royal Commission of inquiry, presided over by Lord Welby. The scope of the Welby Commission was, according to the Madras Congress of 1894, narrowed, and its usefulness limited, because it was not going to conduct an inquiry into the ability of the Indian people to bear their existing financial burdens, but into the financial relations between India and the United Kingdom. A Congress deputation consisting of Wacha, Gokhale, G. Subaramania Iyer, the founder of public life in Madras, and Surendranath Bannerjee proceeded to England to give evidence before this Commission.

While feeling thankful to the Commission for having afforded an opportunity to representative Indians to state the case on behalf of India the Congress urged (1) that the new official members of the Viceroy's Council should be made more directly representative of the Indian people, and that they should have a right to move amendments and divide the Council upon the provisions of the Budget; (2) that military and other unproductive expenditure be reduced, and that larger amounts be spent in promoting the welfare and progress of the people; and (3) that the public Services be Indianized with a view to effecting large savings and more efficient administration.

These demands were considered as extravagant and fantastic by the Anglo-Indian Press. The Government was slow to respond.

This hostility of the Anglo-Indian Press and the indifference of the Government made a section of the Congress indignant and impatient. The repetition of prayers, deputations, and resolutions of the Congress were considered undignified by this section, who felt that agitation hitherto confined only to the educated classes must reach the masses.

When Lord Curzon's appointment as Viceroy was announced the Congress accorded him a "respectful welcome," and hoped that he would follow a policy of progress and confidence in the people. Lord Curzon destroyed the hopes of the Congress with the passing of the Official Secrets Act and the Indian Universities Act. The partition of Bengal was the real climax.

When the Congress met at Bombay in 1904 Sir Pherozeshah Mehta, who was the Chairman of the Reception Committee, exhorted his countrymen to have faith in the "ultimate wisdom, beneficence, and righteousness of the English people." But Bengal did not think that there was such a thing as generosity in John Bull's politics. The Bengalees began to preach the new gospel of self-help. The boycott of British goods was the principal plank in their platform.

When the Congress met at Benares, under the presidency of Gokhale, Bengal and the whole of India were passing through a very anxious period. The official report of the Congress for that year describes the crisis as the darkest since Lord Lytton's Viceroyalty. "India," says the report,

> was the target for so much scorn and calumny emanating from the highest quarters, its most moderate demands ridiculed and scouted, its most reasonable prayers greeted with a stiff negative, its noblest aspirations spurned and denounced as pure mischief, its most cherished ideals hurled down from the pedestal and trodden under foot.

The leaders, who had assembled at Benares from all parts of the country, anxiously considered the critical juncture in the life of the nation. The ideal of colonial self-government, with which the Moderates would be content, was opposed by the impatient idealists, who repudiated the beneficent intentions of the British. The Congress, which was hitherto a homogeneous body, was split into Extremists and Moderates.

The Congress met next year at Surat, where the left and the right wings began by exchanging compliments and ended with blows. The two parted company. The left wing became revolutionary, and resorted to terrorism, which found the most formidable expression in Bengal. The Moderates converted the Congress into a caucus which embodied colonial self-government and constitutional methods in its creed.

Lord Morley lost no time in "rallying the Moderates" by introducing what is known as the Morley-Minto reforms, with the novel feature of a separate and communal representation, which the Congress—henceforward an organ of the Moderates—deprecated on principle. The reforms were not wholly satisfying to the Moderates, though they welcomed what was conceded and decided to give them a fair trial. The Extremists condemned the reforms as a sham, and carried on a campaign out in the country. The Government passed the Seditious Meetings Act and the Press Act, the latter of which received the support of Gokhale. The Extremist campaign was resisted by the Government of Lord Minto and Hardinge, by these special laws, and also by resorting to Regulation III of 1818.

The political agitation was terrific when war broke out. True to its old traditions, however, the Congress leaders said: "England's calamity cannot be India's opportunity. Let the dead past bury its dead." Leading Congressmen co-operated with the Government in maintaining peace and securing recruits. A war measure known as the Defence of India Act was passed with the approval of the leaders of the Indian Legislative Council. Though Lord Hardinge expressly stated that it was "a war measure" meant to deal summarily with the King's enemies, agitators like the Ali brothers and Mrs Annie Besant were interned under that Act. The country protested against these excesses, but still co-operated with the Government. Mahatma Gandhi was busy finding recruits for the Government.

Struck by the loyalty of the Congress, which at the same time stuck to its Home Rule programme, the British Government wisely decided to satisfy the wishes of the people so far as they could, without at the same time relinquishing their real power. At this time the left wing, which had been out of the Congress, was invited by the right wing. A reunited Congress was held at Lucknow in 1916, which also joined hands with the Muslim League to present the amended national demand.

The Secretary of State for India made an announcement on August 20, 1917, promising

> the increasing association of Indians in every branch of the administration, and the gradual development of self-governing institutions with a view to the progressive realization of responsible government in India as an integral part of the British Empire.

The announcement made it clear that progress in this policy can only be achieved by successive stages ; that the British Government and the Government of India, on whom the responsibility lies for the welfare and the advancement of the Indian peoples, must be judges of the time and measure of each advance ; and that they must be guided by the co-operation received from those upon whom new opportunities of service will be conferred, and by the extent to which it is found that confidence may be reposed in their sense of responsibility.

This announcement did not satisfy the Extremists. Still the Congress co-operated with the Montagu Mission.

CHAPTER VI

GANDHI'S WAR ON REFORMS

PARLIAMENT'S pledge of August 20, 1917, embodied *Swaraj*, or responsible government, within the Empire, to which the Montagu-Chelmsford Report gave shape and form. None the less, apprehension existed in the public mind in India that with the close of the War and the passing away of Britain's anxieties in regard to India and the Empire Parliament's enthusiasm for the fulfilment of the promise of self-government might wane. Therefore the political leaders of India took up an uncompromising attitude and spoke of irreducible minimum demands.

The suspicions of "the politically minded classes," to borrow Mr Montagu's phrase, were aggravated by the failure of the late Mr Tilak's action for libel against the late Sir Valentine Chirol. The Press in India freely said that it was difficult to get justice for an Indian from a British jury, and in Britain's eye all agitators were the same, be they constitutionalists or violent rebels.

On the publication of the Montagu-Chelmsford Scheme of constitutional reforms a special session of the Congress was convened which demanded full provincial autonomy, but as a concession to moderate opinion suggested the reservation of law, justice, and police to the existing administration for a period of six years. The Delhi Session of the Indian National Congress in December 1918 insisted on the immediate grant of provincial autonomy, and inserted, in a resolution relating to the dispatch of a deputation to England to appear before the Parliamentary Joint Committee and interview men of consequence in England, a clause binding the delegation to confine negotiations in England strictly to the letter of the resolution passed at Delhi. This restriction of the scope of the activities of the delegates was resented by the Moderates as intolerable interference with the discretion of the plenipotentiaries, who, they maintained, must have a fairly wide charter for negotiation. The Nationalists suspected the Moderates and their passion for compromise. The extremer section attacked their *bona fides*. The breach in the Congress ranks became inevitable. Mrs Besant brought into existence the National Home Rule League, professing views less radical than those which had been approved by the Delhi Congress. The Moderates who seceded from the Congress regrouped themselves under a new banner called the National Liberal Federation.

With the defection of Mrs Besant and her followers and Sir Surendranath Bannerjee and his Moderate associates one might have expected the Congress to become weaker. But the Congressmen carried on an aggressive campaign and identified themselves on tactical grounds with the large body of Mussulmans who had been extremely sensitive about Turkey's future and the mandated territories in the Middle East, where the sacred places of Islam lay. Turkey's sovereign was looked upon as the religious dictator of Islam. If Turkey suffered—in other words, was made to pay for her part in the last War—the Indian Muslim said that the emasculation of the Caliph and the weakening of Islam as a world-force were aimed at.

The over-wrought feelings of the educated classes, united with the despair of the advanced Mohammedans, resulted in a big combination under the Congress. Any Government must have felt the difficulty of the situation and tried to combat it, but the manner of combat offered an opportunity for its opponents, who prepared for resistance. Had the Government relied less on its ancient methods, which ill-suited a reform era, and trusted more to the modern ways of democracy, it would have been obviating instead of increasing its troubles. Its opponents rejoiced, saying: *Quem deus perdere vult, prius dementat.*

There was a real danger of economic discontent becoming a handmaid of political propagandism, because the price of foodstuffs and of clothing, intensified by the failure of the monsoon, added to the sufferings of the middle and lower classes. The Government was held responsible for their woes.

The discontent of the politically minded, the despair of the advanced Mohammedans, and the distress of the masses united in offering battle to the Government of India when it introduced into the Indian Legislative Council the Rowlatt Bills, named after Sir Sidney Rowlatt, the Chairman of the Sedition Committee, which had recommended suppressive legislation.

The Rowlatt Committee had investigated in 1918 the growth of the revolutionary movement in the different provinces of India generally, and especially in Bengal. It had shown that between 1906 and 1918 in that one province alone 311 outrages were committed, over 1000 persons were accused, and 84 convicted. The material before the Committee revealed the extent of the revolutionary organization and the intensity of the revolutionary propaganda conducted in schools and colleges. Up to the period when the War broke out police espionage had been frustrated by revolutionary terrorism, but the activities of the revolutionaries were suspended during the War, as, according to some, they did not want to exploit England's external troubles for India's internal self-government. The Rowlatt Committee, who attributed the cessation of the revolutionary activity mainly to the operation of the Defence of India Act—which was a temporary War measure, like D.O.R.A.—wanted to make it a permanent feature of the Statute Book. The Government, who accepted their view, determined to forge new fetters. This decision plunged the whole country into an open revolutionary struggle, resulting in the Amritsar massacre, martial law in the Punjab, and Mahatma Gandhi's non-violent war.

The first of the two Rowlatt Bills provided for the expeditious trial by a special tribunal consisting of three High Court Judges of all revolutionary offenders, with no right of appeal. Were the Governor-General satisfied that revolutionary activities likely to lead to the commission of offences against the State were widespread further powers could be assumed. In areas where the revolutionary spirit prevailed the Local Governments were to have power to order suspected persons to furnish security, to reside in a particular place, or to abstain from any specified act, or to arrest and to intern them in such places and under such conditions as were prescribed. The purpose of this Bill was to allow the Defence of India Act to continue operating, as its normal period was nearing its end.

Under the second of the Rowlatt Bills, which proposed to make a permanent change in the ordinary criminal law of the land, the possession of a seditious document with the intention to publish or to circulate it was to be punishable with imprisonment, and District Magistrates were empowered to direct police investigation into cases for which under existing law no prosecution could be launched save with the sanction of the Government.

These measures were repudiated by the political parties, both Extremist and Moderate, as "Black Bills." They were condemned as a sinister conspiracy of the Indian Civil Service to neutralize the new spirit which Mr Montagu aspired to introduce into the administration. They were attacked both in and outside the Council as "iron fetters" on India's future progress, the imposition of which would muzzle the Press, chain the platform, and arrest the healthy growth of democracy.

The introduction of the Rowlatt Bills in the February session of the Supreme Legislative Council (1919) raised a hue and cry in the country, the like of which India had not heard since 1857. The Government position was that the passage of the first Bill at least was absolutely necessary for public safety, and must precede any advance along the lines laid down in the Montagu-Chelmsford Scheme. The Government protested their innocence of any design upon the legitimate aspirations of educated India. They were startled at the suspicion aroused in the public mind. Though the Government did not expect any measure of support on a matter calculated to strengthen the hands of the executive from the popular representatives in the Council, the depth of the feeling aroused against the Bill took them aback.

The leaders of India and the Nationalist Press proclaimed that, while the gift of reforms was a sham, repression was a reality. The volume of distrust and racial estrangement became so large that the Government found it impossible to reassure Indian opinion. Had the Government taken courage in both hands, acknowledged public opposition, and withdrawn the Rowlatt Bills the atmosphere would have changed, but the men at the helm felt that their prestige would perish if they did not persist in their ill-starred course.

Sir Chettur Sankaran Nair,[1] who was at this time a member of the Viceroy's Cabinet, was assailed in the European-edited Press for not supporting the Government of India and for his open opposition to Lord Chelmsford, but the fact was that the far-sighted advice of this great stalwart

[1] Sir Chettur Sankaran Nair is one of the great Indians who have occupied high offices under the Crown and fought India's battles as a Radical. As Judge of the Madras High Court for several years, he was noted for his independence and impartiality. Then he became a Member of the Viceroy's Executive Council, which office he resigned in protest against the Government of India's refusal to repudiate Sir Michael O'Dwyer. Then he became a Member of the India Council in London. To-day he is Chairman of the Indian Central Committee, collaborating with the British Parliamentary Commission presided over by Sir John Simon. Sir Chettur Sankaran Nair is universally respected in India, even by his political opponents in the Congress camp.

was not accepted by the Viceroy. When his Excellency assured the Services that the reforms would neither affect their present prospects and position nor their aspirations for the future India suspected that one of the parents of the Montford report was only nailing the lid upon the coffin of his own favourite child.

The atmosphere of suspicion and disgust became thicker and thicker with the prolonged debates on the Rowlatt Bill. In vain did Sir Verney Lovett, himself a member of the Rowlatt Committee, warn the Council of the danger of a revolution which was brewing. The non-officials retorted that the best way to check revolution was to press forward with the reforms, because the revolutionary movement was born of the hunger for national freedom. When healthy food was given in fair quantity there would be no danger. The non-officials felt that the food of reforms was being poisoned with repression.

To cut a long story short, an unprecedented campaign of resistance was set on foot with the passing of the first Rowlatt Act. The Government dropped the second Bill altogether. One wonders to-day why the Government should have passed the measure at all, when it was never put into operation.

The bungling by the Government brought Mr M. K. Gandhi, who had hitherto been a silent but keen spectator of political events after his return from South Africa, to the forefront. Gandhi's readiness to identify himself with the sufferings of the poorer classes had made him a popular hero. Gandhi decided to take up the leadership of the movement, and put into practice his experience in South Africa. Passive resistance, he felt, was the only honourable answer if the Rowlatt Bills were passed in the face of non-official opposition.

Gandhi was as good as his word. Mrs Besant warned the Mahatma that his 'passive resistance' campaign would release forces of evil which he could not control, but Gandhi smiled and ignored her pathetic protest. And before that smile Mrs Besant ceased to be a force in Indian politics. Her influential daily newspaper *New India* rapidly dwindled, only to disappear. Her message was rejected. Gandhi was hailed as India's only Messiah.

By a process of passive resistance of civil laws the Mahatma hoped to compel the Government to abandon the Rowlatt Act. The fact that it was not put into operation has been claimed as his partial success by his associates.

The new era of *satyagraha*, or passive resistance, was inaugurated with a pledge to the effect that its signatories would refuse civilly to obey the Rowlatt Act and such other laws as the committee to be thereafter appointed might think fit, and, further, that in the struggle they would faithfully follow truth and refrain from violence to life, person, or property.

The Mahatma had the advantage of a sympathetic Legislature, in which non-official opposition warmly supported him. Thus both in and outside the Council the Indian voice was united and unanimous in its denouncement of the Rowlatt Act. The educated classes had no doubt now that the era of reforms had yielded place to 'repression.' They appealed to the masses, whose response was ready and daring.

This is the first time in the history of India when the leaders seriously approached the masses. Politics were hitherto confined to the educated classes. Henceforward the masses were destined to take a lively part in them. That, indeed, was the deliberate purpose of the reforms. By a strange irony it was dangerously fulfilled by the Rowlatt Act.

A wild and fervid propaganda was preached against a perverse and reactionary Government. The Government met propaganda by counter-propaganda. All the resources of the Government were fully used to prevent the politician from capturing the mass mind. Thousands of copies of the Act were distributed. Important official pronouncements as to the "harmless character" of the new Act were communicated to the people in *darbars*.

Gandhi called on the country to observe a *hartal* (day of general strike) on April 16, which was so spontaneous and so successful that it caused confusion among the officials. Not accustomed to general strikes unaccompanied by riots and bloodshed, the Anglo-Indian Press called for resolute government. The *hartal*, they said, was the harbinger of red ruin.

Staggered by the rebellion of the people, Sir Michael O'Dwyer, the Lieutenant-Governor of the Punjab, deported two prominent leaders of Amritsar, and resisted the march of Mahatma Gandhi himself to the battle-front in the Punjab. "The arrest of the Mahatma," as the papers described his expulsion from the Punjab, was the match which fired the magazine. Mobs demonstrated their frenzy. Disturbances followed in Amritsar. The civil authority felt unequal to the situation. General Dyer, who was asked to intervene, produced "sufficient moral effect from a military point of view," and subsequently the Government enforced martial law in certain selected areas in the Punjab.

The gulf of estrangement between the Europeans and Indians widened. His Majesty the King attempted to bridge it by issuing an amnesty. The leaders of the Indian National Congress which met a few weeks later in Amritsar (December 1919) tried to take a reasonable view, but their followers were exasperated. The President of the Congress, Pundit Motilal Nehru, advised the young men not to boycott the reforms, but to work them for what they were worth. He said: "The Act is not based on the wishes of the people of India, and its provisions fall short of the minimum demands made by the Congress. But let us not belittle the good that the Act does us." The Pundit, however, has never been a man of strong conviction. He presently became potter's clay in the hands of his extremist son.

"The physical son," exclaimed a critic, "became the political father."

As if the exasperation caused by the Punjab tragedy was not enough, Muslim sentiment was shocked by the treatment meted out to Turkey and the Khalifat. Mr Lloyd George, then the Prime Minister, made a solemn declaration on January 6, 1918, which included the following pledge: "Nor are we fighting to deprive Turkey of its capital or of the rich and renowned lands of Asia Minor and Thrace which are predominantly Turkish in race." When the War was over it was fast becoming clear that the British Prime Minister was not going to fulfil his pledged word.

The state of things in the Near East was far from encouraging. The Mussulmans of India were asking:

> With Arabia independent, with foreign Powers governing Mesopotamia, Syria, and Armenia, in the guise of the mandatories, with Palestine restored to the Jews, with the Greeks securely lodged in Smyrna and the Hinterland, what may we ask is the position of the Khalifat?

The Muslim Press and public made it clear that the Khalifat was the very essence of Islam, and its temporal and spiritual strength and importance should remain intact. The Muslims declined to participate in the peace celebrations, from which the Hindus also abstained in deference to the feelings of their brothers in adversity. The anti-Turkish organs in the Christian countries plainly demanded the expulsion of Turkey bag and baggage from Constantinople.

Even moderate Mussulmans were considerably perturbed by this attitude of hostility. A deputation waited on the Viceroy, who in turn assured them that his Government were doing their utmost to impress on his Majesty's Government that Indian Muslim opinion and sentiment should receive their most sympathetic attention before any final settlement could be arrived at with the Allies in regard to Turkey and her dominions. The advanced Muslims treated this as mere 'lip-sympathy,' and called on the community not to be misled by words which were not substantiated by deeds.

The postponement of the publication of the Draft Peace Terms only created further suspicion in the minds of the Muslim community, which was by this time united in its desire that Turkey should not be dismembered and that the Khalifat should retain the same old prestige and power. These Muslims felt that the Viceroy did not appreciate fully the gravity of the issue or the depth of Indian Muslim feeling.

Speaking to the members of the Indian Legislative Council at the end of January 1920, the Viceroy hoped that the present agitation was but a passing phase. "There may be clouds in our sky," said Lord Chelmsford, "but the shadows they cast are relieved by much that is bright." His plea was that the group of politicians who were enthusiastic about the reforms should "set up a bulwark of sanity and moderation against the forces of disorder and destruction." The words of the Viceroy met with a response from the Moderates. "Let us live together in peace and amity," said Sir Surendranath Bannerjee, "in the cultivation of those friendly relations which alone can make for our mutual advantage and mutual prosperity. We, the educated Indians, are prepared to extend the hand of fellowship and friendship to the servants of the Government, to the representatives of the European community."

The Congress was displeased with the attitude of the Moderates in the Council Chamber.

Muslim feeling was getting more and more exerted over the Khalifat question. A Khalifat deputation headed by Maulana Mohammed Ali proceeded to England. The messages that it sent from time to time only intensified the extreme solicitude of he Mussulmans. The interview between the Prime Minister and the Khalifat deputation added fuel to the fire. Mr Lloyd George was frankly disappointing. Mr Mohammed Ali informed the country that he was more and more convinced that the battle of the Khalifat had to be fought on Indian soil.

Maulana Shaukat Ali issued a manifesto that the Mussulmans could be no longer loyal to England when that loyalty clashed with their faithful adherence to the Khalifat. Gandhi proclaimed that March 19, 1920, would be observed as a day of national mourning in the Khalifat cause. In a manifesto which he published on March 10 the Mahatma plainly stated his intentions if the Khalifat demands were not granted: "The barbarous method is warfare open or secret. This must be ruled out not only because it is impracticable." The civilized method was non-violent non-co-operation, on which he courageously and deliberately launched the country.

This made the Government anxious. They decided to combat the observance of the Khalifat day by passing a resolution prohibiting Government servants from participating in it. This caused quite a commotion among the Mussulmans.

When the country was thus seething with indignation the report of the Congress Commission on the Punjab disturbances saw the light of day. Its revelations were gruesome. The Congress Commissioners recommended certain measures necessary for redressing the wrong done to the people, for the purification of the administration, and for preventing a repetition in future of "official lawlessness." They demanded the repeal of the Rowlatt Act, the relieving of Sir Michael O'Dwyer of any responsible office under the Crown, the relieving of all guilty officers and officials of any position of responsibility under the Crown, the dismissal of minor officials charged with corrupt practice on proof of their guilt, the recall of the Viceroy, and the refund of fines and remission of all indemnity.

When the Punjab report was being furiously discussed in the Press and on the platform the Turkish peace terms were announced. The publication of the draft terms of the Turkish peace in May was treated by the entire Muslim community as a deliberate violation of a pledge on the part of the Prime Minister. The Government of India knew that the peace terms must be cruelly disappointing to the Muslims. The Viceroy sympathized with them, saying that the peace included " terms which must be painful to all Muslims." His Excellency also complimented the Muslims on " the splendid response " made by them " in the days of the Empire's needs." He expressed the hope that the old friendship of England and Turkey would revive, and in that hope appealed to the Mussulmans to accept the peace terms with resignation, courage, and fortitude, and to keep their loyalty toward the Crown bright and untarnished, as it had been for so many generations.

Matters became distinctly worse for the Government when the report of the Hunter Committee was published. It was divided on racial lines. In their dissenting minutes the Indian members established that there was no justification for the introduction of martial law, as the disturbances could have been suppressed without abrogation of civil authority. The Government tried to relieve the prevailing tension by expressing its genuine sympathy for those who had suffered.

Neither the views and findings of the Government of India on the Hunter Report nor the pronouncement of his Majesty's Government, which was strong in its disapproval of General Dyer's action, could satisfy the Indian people. The least that the Government could have done to soften acerbities, said the Congress politician, would have been to enforce the minimum demands of the Congress Commissioners.

The Indian Press attacked the Government with unprecedented bitterness. The Anglo-Indian Press treated Indian opinion with disdain. A section of the British Press paid flattering tribute to General Dyer as the " saviour of the British Empire in India." The English and the Anglo-Indian admirers of Dyer opened a fund as a protest against the Government's censure of the General, and liberally contributed to it. When the Punjab question came up for discussion in the House of Lords the Congress felt that the House virtually supported Dyer. The attitude of the Anglo-Indian and British community and that of the House of Lords was considered by the Nationalist Press as an insult of the first magnitude and an index of the mentality of the rulers of the land.

A conference was convened at Allahabad (June 3, 1920) of the representative Indian leaders of all parties and creeds to consider the crucial situation. A committee was appointed, with Gandhi as its guiding spirit, to ascertain and enforce the wish of the nation in regard to non-co-operation. A special session of the Congress was held at Calcutta in September 1920. The reforms since embodied in an Act of Parliament had no attraction for the delegates, all of whom recognized that it had no power either to right the Khalifat or to prevent a repetition of the Punjab wrongs.

Leaders like Pal and Das advocated at the Congress the capture of the Councils. They did so, they explained, with a view not to co-operate with the bureaucracy, but to obstruct its work and to paralyse the Legislature. This programme of obstruction was considered as too mild by Gandhi and his followers, among whom was Pundit Motilal Nehru. The Congress voted for rebellion.

Armed revolt was out of the question. To some it was beyond the range of practical politics; others were opposed to it on principle. Muslim feeling was considerably exercised. Over 18,000 Mussulmans had already gone on *Hijrat* to Afghanistan, like the Pilgrim Fathers. The Special Congress decided to embark on a course of non-co-operation. Das opposed it, and felt deeply that his programme should have been rejected without a trial. Motilal Nehru chuckled with delight over the defeat of Das and Council entry.

Gandhi was intransigent. His large mass following secured for him a narrow majority in the Congress. But the best minds of India, the intelligentsia of the whole country, voted against the boycott of the Councils, by adopting which they felt that they would be boycotting themselves. Gandhi's victory was a triumph of the proletariat over the educated middle classes, who subsequently defeated the mass movement of the non-co-operators by supporting the British Government. Das had the better of logic in the debate, but Gandhi the magic and the votes.

Gandhi in his orations predicted that at the forthcoming elections not a single individual would go to the polls. Das contended that it was impossible, as there would be always some people to go to the polls. Gandhi argued that the mind of the voters must be taken away from the Councils. Das answered that the Indians in the Councils would be a moral support to the Government. Gandhi pointed out that if the majority of the voters did not exercise their votes the Councils would have no more moral sanction left. Das replied that the abstinence of the voters from the exercise of their franchise was not a sure test of the hold of the Congress on the masses, for the simple reason that even in the most advanced countries a large number of voters never cared to go to the polls. Gandhi pleaded that the reforms would thrive on their entry into the Councils. Das retorted that they would follow a policy of persistent obstruction and, if the Government did not respond, paralyse the Legislature. Gandhi maintained that reforms would flourish on obstruction, as every Legislature must have an opposition; the more militant the opposition, the better it would be for the Legislature. With his poetic originality and devastating brilliance Das argued that in every self-governing country the majority accepted office, but he would force the pace of self-government by capturing a majority of seats, refusing the salaries of Ministers, censuring the Government, and suspending dyarchy and the Legislature itself, even as the Duma was suspended in the Russia of the Tsars. Gandhi feared that his scheme of non-co-operation would suffer. Das foretold with prophetic wisdom that precipitate non-co-operation would land the Congress in a fiasco, but a preliminary campaign to paralyse one department, the legislative department of the Government and the Legislature itself, the success of which was as certain as their securing the majority of seats in the Legislatures, would be a bright prelude to non-co-operation if the Government failed to respond.

The country was wholly with the Extremists. Not one single Moderate would have been returned to the Legislature. The Congress was at the height of its power. But Gandhi was obdurate. Das vainly appealed to the Mahatma to give him a chance for a year; if the General Elections of 1920 were missed they would not have a similar opportunity for another three years.

When the General Elections of 1923 came Das had his way, but then the times had changed. Some of the best and most influential workers of the Congress had been disqualified, having undergone a period of more than six months' imprisonment, which, as the law then stood, prevented them from offering themselves as candidates. Some others were still rotting in prison. The spirit of many others had been broken by repression. And the failure of the Mahatma's policy had demoralized the workers, disillusioned the masses, and created internal discord, the inevitable concomitant of loss of faith. The programme of Das was never given a good chance. This painful feeling, which continued to the last day of his life, was known to some of his friends, of whom the present writer was one.

The Dassites felt, and still feel, that had Gandhi possessed his soul in patience for one year—if his Tolstoyan principles had forbidden him from taking part in working out Das's scheme—the Legislatures all over the land would have been captured and the Government forced to yield. The Moderates, the moral support of the Government, who tempted them with office and power to smash the non-co-operation movement, would have been compelled either to retire from politics or to throw in their lot with the Extremists.

Das felt that the policy of Montagu was the same as that of Morley. Lord Morley had said: " Rally the Moderates." Das paraphrased this formula as *Divide et impera.*

The rallying process succeeded. The Moderate felt he was somebody as a member of the Government. Frequent dinners in Government Houses and easy familiarity with lords and ladies who were hitherto inaccessible to him turned his head. He felt that the strength of the Government was his own. And the Government felt that without the Moderates they would have been isolated. Mutual admiration could go no further. The crushing of the non-co-operation movement followed. The rout of Gandhi, the imprisonment of Das, the arrest of Lajpat Rai, and the incarceration of their numerous followers—numbering about twenty thousand—were achievements of which the Moderates were proud.

Nothing succeeds like successful repression! Pundit Motilal Nehru, one of the principal lieutenants of Gandhi, soon after his release from prison transferred his allegiance to Das. Pundit and Patel wrote the report of the Civil Disobedience Committee, postponing Civil Disobedience to the Greek Kalends. Until the passing away of C. R. Das the wily Pundit of Allahabad preached obstruction to satisfy his chief and his wild henchmen, but all the time planned co-operation. He was anxious to return to the pleasant and sheltered paths and cultivate the English officials. Six months' course in the Lucknow Gaol had broken the Pundit's spirit. He was converted to the creed of Council entry, if not obstruction.

The failure of the non-co-operation movement won for Das a large support among the non-co-operators themselves. Rendered weak by fate and premature non-co-operation, the Congress camp was rent asunder by squabbles. A band of irreconcilables continued to attack Das. The malicious organs of the Congress would have his head on a charger.

Had India followed Das, and not Gandhi, three years earlier the history of Indian nationalism would have been differently written. The country would not have been led into a morass. Das was a born fighter, imbued with an Englishman's spirit of freedom; he was in that sense Anglicized to the core. Add the bulldog will of an Englishman to the Celtic emotionalism of the Bengalee, and you get an idea of the late C. R. Das. He was, without exaggeration, a combination of all that was best in Arthur Griffith, Lord Fisher, and Lord Haldane, in one word, a philosopher-statesman-of-action. Gandhi appealed to the imagination of the masses, to whom the name of a Mahatma had a fascination. Added to his 'Mahatma-ship' was his rural simplicity, which impressed the crowds more than the grandeur of C. R. Das's princely style of living. The Mahatma forgot that the masses could not be controlled without the leadership of the classes, especially as his programme was one of prolonged suffering and spiritual non-violence, rather than of militant political aggression. Gandhi was for experiments in non-violence, calling on the people to immolate themselves at the altar of *satya* ("truth"). Gandhi had great faith in the Englishman, whom Das approached with frank distrust, not because the Englishman as such was made of stone which would not relent at untold suffering, but because India was not concerned with the Englishman as such, but a steel frame of the bureaucracy. Their fight was not with men, felt Das, but with the very machine. Both Das and Gandhi wanted to paralyse the machine, but their method was different. Gandhi in his impatience and distrust of C. R. Das—which the Mahatma once publicly owned—did not give Das a chance. The Bengalee giant could have fought Gandhi to a finish, but such a course, he felt, would strengthen the stranger within the gate. So Das sank his convictions—unlike the Liberals—before the mob-mentality of the Mahatma, and, instead of leading, followed.

When Das attempted to revive his old policy of obstruction after the overthrow of non-co-operation he was setting his hand to a task which even Hercules would have hesitated to take up. With the Congress Party split from brow to chin there was not the ghost of a chance of their securing a majority in the Legislatures. But to the credit of Das be it said that even with the help of a minority he succeeded in successfully obstructing the dyarchy and finally suspending it in Bengal. With the help of their Mohammedan allies the Bengal Swarajists defeated the Government at the beginning of 1924 on a series of resolutions relating to the political prisoners and repressive legislation. They scored several successes during the Budget debate, and rejected many grants for Reserved as well as Transferred subjects, including the Ministers' salaries. The Ministers, however, decided to serve without salaries until the question could be resubmitted to the Council! The vote for the salaries of Ministers was put to the Council again some months later and was again defeated. The result was that dyarchy had to be suspended temporarily in Bengal.

CHAPTER VII

THE PROVINCIAL COUNCILS

THE temporary suspension of dyarchy in Bengal and the Central Provinces was an interruption to political progress in one sense and a stimulation to it in another. It disturbed the smooth work of the reforms. It tried to kill the tender growth. Moderate elements in the country deplored obstruction as doing incalculable harm. Their powerful campaign revived the faith of the people in constitutional progress on well-regulated lines, a faith which proved so infectious that the Extremists in the Legislatures who had come " to scoff remained to pray." Well might the Government claim that

> a variety of reasons, of which undoubtedly one of the most potent was the growing aversion of the electorates from a policy of pure negation, had compelled the Swarajists to abandon their purely wrecking policy and, even, on occasions, to co-operate with the Government.[1]

On the very rock of obstruction the Swaraj Party floundered. A ferocious section of it accepted office !

An outstanding feature of the working of the reforms in the Provincial Councils was the devotion of the Ministers to the task of nation-building. On local self-government, primary education, rural co-operation, agricultural development, and the like, parties in the Councils ranged on opposite sides. Such differences of opinion on things of vital importance to the public welfare proved healthy.

There could not be any uniformity of policy or progress

[1] *India in 1925 and 1926*, by J. Coatman, Director of Public Information, Government of India.

in the various provinces. Different provinces progressed along different lines, and advanced at varying speed.

Dyarchy broke down in two provinces. In others it failed to satisfy the growing aspiration for power, and in this very dissatisfaction lay its success. For dyarchy was not meant to succeed as a permanent feature of Indian reforms. It was a preparatory stage, a training school for politicians. The impatient ones did not attend the class. The patient ones passed the examination. But both the truants and the earnest students have contributed in their conflicting ways to constitutional stability, which has come to stay in the provinces.

Under dyarchy the dominating personality in the provinces was not the Minister, or the Executive Councillor, but the Governor of the province. He was something more than a *deus ex machina*. He was no doubt the saviour of the situation in a semi-revolutionary crisis. But his control extended to routine business and small affairs of departmental policy. Not only the Executive Councillors and Ministers bring their more important problems before him, but the permanent heads of departments, both Transferred and Reserved, approach him often to acquaint him with all the affairs of their departments. No officer of an Imperial Service can be transferred from one district or from one appointment to another without his consent.

The Governor's control over his Ministers has been unrestricted in theory and in practice. Under the constitution the Governor can direct action to be taken in regard to the administration of the Transferred departments otherwise than in accordance with the advice of his Ministers. The Ministers have frequently resented the excessive control exercised by the Governor over them.[1] The Governors have not made any endeavours to accept the position of a constitutional head.

[1] See the evidence of ex-Ministers before the Reforms Inquiry Committee, of which the late Sir Alexander Muddiman was the Chairman.

Partly because of the traditions and partly because of the difficulties of dyarchy the Governor has acted throughout as the executive head of the province. The Governor has had to play the dual *rôle* of a Governor and a Prime Minister. The Ministers, by submitting to his rulings in the latter capacity, have shown that it is not always that a Minister resigns when he differs from his chief.

One inevitable difficulty in the provinces arose from the impinging on each other of the Reserved and the Transferred departments. This was avoided so far as possible. Instances are not wanting of ample opportunity being afforded for the exercise of influence by Ministers over the administration of Reserved subjects.

In Madras, during the first two and half years of dyarchy, out of 121 meetings of the Government 114 were joint deliberations of Executive Councillors and Ministers, and only seven separate meetings of the Executive Council were held.

In Bengal, too, the Madras practice was followed. To begin with, the Governor dealt with the Executive Councillors in charge of the Reserved subjects. Then he dealt with the Ministers and their departments separately. Then he arranged Cabinet meetings of the Ministers and Executive Councillors, at which the Budget and the general provincial policy were discussed.

Thus, when dyarchy was being assailed by non-cooperation outside, the two halves of the Government, acting together, not only increased their strength, but also succeeded in putting down their common opponents with a heavy hand.

In the Central Provinces all important matters of policy were discussed at joint meetings.

In the Punjab weekly meetings were held of the Ministers and the Executive Councillors. An account of the relations between both sides of the Government by one of them who has, after retirement, joined the Socialist Party in England may be quoted. Sir John Maynard, who was the Finance Member of the Punjab Governor's Executive Council, wrote:

> During the first three years of the reforms there were occasions when a member of the Executive Council and a Minister sitting together arrived at important decisions on questions of urgency, in the absence on tour of the rest of the Government. I recollect one such important decision on a matter affecting the Sikh problem in November 1921. It was arrived at by the Minister of Agriculture and myself. The Minister of Agriculture and I also conducted jointly certain conversations with Sikhs in November and December 1922, with the object of finding a solution of the differences regarding shrines legislation. My own impression of the relations between Members and Ministers and between Minister and Minister during the lifetime of the first Council is that they were most cordial and friendly. There were only three cases in which the Ministers stood together as against the Executive Councillors. In one case the Ministers agreed together in taking a more uncompromising view of the obligation of maintaining law and order than the two Executive Councillors were prepared to take. On a second occasion during the preparation of the Budget of 1923–24 the Government of India declined to finance a substantial deficit, and reduction had to be made. The Ministers stood together against the Finance Department in objecting to reductions in the Transferred departments. The matter was temporarily arranged by consent of all. Then a further demand for the reduction of expenditure by some 60 lakhs was made by the Government of India. The Governor sitting with his Members and Ministers commissioned the Finance Member to select the items for reduction, with the result that proposed expenditure in all departments was drastically curtailed. Neither Minister protested against this. On a third occasion, not of great importance, the Ministers took one view and the Members another on some proposals of the President of the Punjab Legislative Council for the treatment of reports of Select Committees.
>
> Sometimes we had the two Ministers standing with either

one Executive Councillor or the other against the second Councillor. They stood with the Sikh Executive Councillor against the Member for Finance on the question of a permanent Public Service Commission, which appeared to threaten patronage. They agreed with the Finance Member against the Revenue Member on an important question of taxation. They agreed with the Revenue Member against the Finance Member in their attitude towards the elected Standing Committees of the House and the publication of their proceedings.

Perhaps the most difficult and troublesome question which has been before Government in these years was the question of the Sikh shrines. There were very numerous discussions with all parties concerned, and a number of projects of law were prepared. Technically the subject was a Transferred subject, in the control of a Minister, but questions of law and order were closely involved. The unitary character of the administration can best be gauged by the manner in which this group of problems were dealt with. Up to November 1922, when the Gurdwara Bill which ultimately became law was introduced into the Council, no difference of principle revealed itself between the Members of the Government. This was not because there was no joint consultation, for there were very frequent meetings and discussions between all of us on the subject. If there had been differences they had not been stated, and it is naturally assumed that when a man does not say that he differs he does not attach enough importance to the difference to contest the point. The Bill of November 1922 was in all essential particulars identical in principle with that of March 1921, though in one or two points of detail slightly more favourable to the contentions of the reforming Sikhs. On the Bill of March 1921 no differences between the Members of the Government had disclosed themselves. But when the Bill of November 1922 was introduced, two changes of circumstance had occurred. On the one hand, the claims of the reforming Sikhs had risen for reasons into which it is unnecessary to enter here. On the other hand, the difference between the Muslim and Hindu Communities, quiescent before, had become acute and had culminated in destructive riots. Hindus, alarmed, were looking for an ally, and held out to Sikhs the hope of a favourable settlement by consent. Hindus and Sikhs combined to resist Government's Bill, the former because it went too far, and the latter because it did not go far enough, and feeling was so strong that it became extremely difficult for any man to stand against the sentiment of his own section of the community. In the voting on the Bill there was a division between the Members of the Government. One Executive Member and one Minister voted for the Bill. One Executive Councillor and one Minister abstained from voting. But the two latter did not feel strongly enough on the subject, when the Bill was passed, to resign their posts, and they continued to co-operate cordially with the other members of the Government in the measures, which were at once resumed, for bringing about a settlement of the Sikh question.

The above observations of Sir John Maynard go to show the way in which the Ministers were identified with the administration of their province. A better instance could hardly be cited of the partnership of the Ministers in the business of the Government than the manner in which opportunities were given to them to influence the Government in a matter of serious public importance.

In the United Provinces there was joint consultation of the two halves in regard to the peasant revolt in four districts. The Governor-in-Council, acting with his Ministers, Pundit Jagat Narain and Mr C. Y. Chintamani, applied the Seditious Meetings Act to the affected districts. The Ministers courageously supported what their critics denounced as repression. Eight years after the Swarajists made common cause with these very ex-Ministers and their associates in regard to their plans of constitution-making. This incident again shows that the Ministers have not shirked their responsibility to maintain law and order when the necessity for it arises, even at the risk of incurring public opposition, which is only temporary and leaves no lasting spite.

The question of joint responsibility of the Ministers has not worked in any other province so satisfactorily as in the United Provinces, where the Minister for local self-government carried it to a point of resigning over a question which affected his colleague, but with which he had no concern.

The same principle, however, could not be applied in a Muslim province like the Punjab, where on a question of joint responsibility both the Muslim and the Hindu Ministers are bound to resign on principle. But practical considerations would make the application of that principle impossible. The Punjab is a communal province. The Hindu Minister, in a Bill dealing with money-lenders, who are mostly Hindus, would have no other alternative but to resign if he feels that the Bill is aimed at his community. But the Muslim Minister cannot resign, because his community will claim that the Bill is meant for their benefit.

Under responsible government, in certain provinces, one must be prepared for a reign of communal parties at least for some time. Communalism is an enemy of responsible government. But responsibility alone can be its cure. The obvious plea of the Simon Commission for not recommending Dominion status for the whole of India will be that the communities have hopelessly failed to adjust their differences, and no common formula has been found even between the Nehrus and the Jinnahs, the so-called Nationalists among the communities.

Notwithstanding the deplorable differences of a communal character it must be admitted that the wiser heads in the various communities have always discouraged the laying of too much emphasis on them. A perusal of the proceedings of the Provincial and the Central Legislatures will convince one as to how political, economic, financial, and other matters dominate the various discussions.

The Provincial Councils have seldom missed an opportunity to assert their influence in regard to financial matters.

The police in all the Provincial Councils are the subject of vehement attack every year. The non-official Opposition succeeds in making cuts on police grants every year. The Budget discussions in the Provincial Councils are an index of the interest that the public take in the financial administration of the country. And when these discussions are directed along reasonable and practical channels the Government have not been unwilling to listen. Let us mention a few instances.

A resolution moved in the Bengal Council asking the Government of India that special consideration be granted to Bengal's financial difficulties resulted in the temporary remission of Bengal's annual contribution to the Central Exchequer.

In Bihar and Orissa the Government accepted a resolution of the non-official members for the appointment of a committee to review the whole system of primary and secondary education, and two years later the same Council adopted a resolution definitely committing itself to the ideal of universal free and compulsory education.

In the Punjab several of the important non-official resolutions relating to the Transferred subjects, ranging from the establishment of a Provincial Co-operative Bank to the adoption of measures to improve milch-cows, were given effect to by the Local Government.

Here it must be candidly admitted that many of the non-official resolutions are sheer rubbish. Were the Councils entrusted with the responsibilities of self-government they would either not have been moved or only moved as a joke to relieve the boredom of the Legislature. The innumerable interpellations indulged in by the Members indicate their desire to swell the pages of the Council reports, and they derive consolation from looking up the index to see how busy they have been. Most of the interpellations are matters more for a District Board or a village *panchayat* than for the Provincial Council. As the Council has no power of removing the Government, the Congress members have been in the habit of treating it as a farce. The more responsible members and parties, however, have confined their questions to administrative policy or practice. The Government have never hesitated to deal with responsible motions in a responsible manner. When with the reshaping of the reforms the provinces are invested with increased responsibility there can be no doubt whatever that the Opposition will also become more responsible. Irresponsibility is the privilege of all Oppositions, even when it means that they will one day be called to office, but when there is no such provision in the statute there is naturally no inducement to restraint.

One of the most important results of the introduction of partial responsibility in the provinces is the relaxation of the control of the Government of India. So far as Transferred departments are concerned, their interference has been reduced to a minimum. With the control of the purse the Councils in the provinces will be able to improve the condition of the rural masses, who constitute the bulk of the population.

Living mostly in tiny hamlets made up of mud-huts, or in lonely shielings on mountain-sides and river-banks, where no civilizing influence penetrates, where the march of progress which has touched the cities has never ventured to reach, where newspapers seldom find their way, save when a schoolmaster in one of the bigger villages, or a priest, reads aloud to them, where news itself comes in the shape of a terrific rumour wafted by the winds, the masses of rural population have remained unchanged from the days when Emperor Asoka ruled over them ages ago. Were Alexander the Great to come to India he would recognize it as the India he saw. But were he to visit his own homeland he would not recognize it.

Even a century and a half of British rule has not changed the aspect or the outlook of the villages. The Reformed

Councils have failed to affect them, because they have not produced parties with an effective programme for the amelioration of rural conditions. Such a programme cannot be produced by serious-minded politicians so long as they have not the power, if they secure a majority, to enforce their will. Only responsible government in the provinces can produce Parliamentary parties such as one finds in the advanced countries of Europe. It is easy to deplore the absence of well-conceived policies consistently carried out for ten years of reforms. No lasting policy can be conceived by parties so long as they are not entrusted with the power to carry it out. It is cheap to say that so long as communal dissensions exist true parties cannot be, but it would be more true to point out that communalism cannot die so long as political parties have no chance to thrive—and political parties cannot thrive in the absence of a responsible Parliamentary system. It is absolutely certain that, entrusted with powers, the time will soon come when rabid communalism will hide its diminished head.

While the critics who attribute the absence of parties to the prevalence of a communal spirit are wrong it cannot be denied that communalism has been introduced into the Councils by men who should have known that that was hardly the way to serve the nation's cause.

The communal tendency is apt to be exaggerated. That it is not an insuperable obstacle in the way of the development of Parliamentary institutions must be patent from the fact that a good deal of legislative work has been done in which all communities have taken keen interest.

Real public interest in the provinces centred round local self-government, the regulation of municipalities, and District Boards. There are 757 municipalities in British India, but only eighteen million inhabitants out of two hundred and fifty million live in them. Of these, Bombay, Madras, and Calcutta hold more than three millions. The remaining municipalities are much smaller.

In the United Provinces the Minister for local self-government devoted his energy and ability to the reconstruction of the units of local self-government, both urban and rural. The District Boards, whose chairmen used to be the District Magistrates, were henceforth to be presided over by non-officials; official control yielded place to non-official control. Direct elections were introduced in the District Boards, as in the Legislatures. The number of votes was increased, and franchise was lowered. Similar progress was made all over the country. In Madras, for instance, local bodies may now impose taxes on amusements and entertainments.

The *panchayats* of old (communities of elders) were revived in various provinces. The *panchayats* were invested with definite powers. The Punjab Panchayat Act empowers the committee to settle local disputes and undertake measures for the sanitation of the villages. The United Provinces Act enables them to deal with petty civil suits and to settle minor cases under the Cattle Trespass Act and the Village Sanitation Act. In Bihar and Orissa, and in Bengal, the *panchayats* have powers to create village unions and constitute Union Boards on an elective basis, whose functions are more or less like those of the Parish Councils in England. The *panchayats* are popular in the Madras Presidency. The one difficulty in the successful working of these *panchayats* is the strong objection of the villagers to the taxation imposed by them.

Increased interest in local self-government is evidenced by the formation of the rate-payers' associations in various parts of India. Elections to District Boards and municipalities create an even greater interest than elections to the Councils.

Some provincial administration reports say that in municipal administration efficiency has suffered. The answer to that is that popular satisfaction has increased. Democracy may not be efficient, but it gives satisfaction to the people.

Another subject which occupied the constant attention of the Provincial Council was education, a Transferred subject. The results would have been satisfactory had funds been available. There are roughly six and three-quarter millions studying in the primary schools, and one and a quarter million in secondary schools. The curse of the educational system in India is that it is top-heavy. The students who complete their educational courses, which are of a literary kind, become professors, clerks, or Deputy Collectors, but not business men. The higher education is not broad-based on primary education. Men with a technical bent of mind have no facilities or opportunities in the schools. Physical culture is neglected. The population of Bengal is nearly equal to that of the United Kingdom, but the percentage of students taking full-time university courses is about ten times as great as the percentage in England, whereas only about 4 per cent. of the total population in 1923 was receiving education, including primary education.

The reformed Councils have not made any headway toward providing on a vast scale facilities for technical education. Primary education has not been expanded as it ought to be. The plea that teachers are not available for primary education is absurd in face of a bewildering growth of unemployment among the educated middle classes. It is said that teachers would not be available in the country itself for some time for technical schools. If given an attractive salary, experts can be imported from foreign countries. Further, the services of many Indians who are rotting for want of jobs, after undergoing technical courses abroad, could be utilized.

The problem of women's education presents peculiar difficulties. In Upper India medieval superstition persists, though in several enlightened families the education of girls is not neglected. With the gradual increase in the education of girls the want of woman teachers is tending to decrease. The age-old prejudices of *purdah*, which are alien to Aryan

India, but a legacy of Muslim rule, are being slowly conquered.

More money is wanted to meet the increasing enthusiasm for education. More money can be had by a policy of increased taxation and greater economy in administration. Without the responsibility of administration leaders have naturally shown a disinclination to support bureaucratic proposals for increased taxation.

With all these handicaps it is pleasing to note that since the introduction of reforms there has been tangible progress in compulsory primary education. Municipalities have faced the responsibilities of increased taxation so far as they can in a country where people are very poor. The Ministerial policy of decentralization of the control of primary education has made many a municipality levy maximum taxation to find funds for education. After three years of the working of the reforms the number of pupils receiving education had increased by one million.

Regarding secondary education, every endeavour is being made to see to it that it is as complete as possible. In a number of provinces Boards for secondary and intermediate education and intermediate colleges, which are being set up, may be expected gradually to supply the need for vocational instruction, the lack of which is one of the great defects of Indian education at the present time.

Night classes for mill-workers and women, though few in number, show that there is a desire to provide for the education of the adult illiterates.

An idea of the enthusiasm for education which the Reformed Government has shown may be gathered from Sir John Maynard's evidence before the Muddiman Committee in 1924, which relates to the backward provinces of the Punjab.

> The period of the Reformed Government has been characterized by a very remarkable development in primary education. During the first three years of the Reformed

Administration the number of pupils in primary schools rose from 239 to 351 thousands, an increase of 47 per cent.; and the percentage of persons under instructions to total population is now 4·07 as against 2·7 before the reforms. This increase in numbers has been accompanied by a substantial advance towards the abolition of the efficient one-teacher schools, which have been replaced, to the number of 1250, by two-teacher schools. There has been a steady advance in the application of the principle of compulsion, under the Enabling Act of 1919. . . . In a number of other areas, where compulsion has not been applied, societies of parents, organized under the auspices of the Department of Co-operative Credit, have bound themselves, under penalty, to send their children to school for the full four years' primary course. There has been an increase of 18 per cent. in the number of pupils in secondary schools; and of 27 per cent. in the number of girls undergoing instruction of all kinds. The number of teachers trained annually has risen in the triennium from 2235 to 3225—that is, by 44 per cent. A further movement towards the reduction of illiteracy has been inaugurated by the Ministry of Education in the establishment of schools for adults, of whom there are now over 40,000 undergoing instruction. The aggregate increase in three years in the number of persons receiving instruction is 150,000, nearly twice as great as the greatest increase in any other Indian province. In the region of Higher Education, the completion of the University Chemical Laboratory, the opening of the Maclagan College for Mechanical Engineering, the establishment of five Intermediate Colleges for men and one for women, are among the achievements of the Ministry. These facts show what can be done, under a so-called dyarchical system, in a period of financial stress, by a judicious enthusiasm and a courageous perseverance.

The progress made may be regarded as vast in view of the brief space of time and the financial difficulty, but it does not touch the fringe of the large masses of population, who are still illiterate. The chief handicap has been want of funds.

H

After local self-government and education comes the vexed question of industrial development. Every province has its Department of Industries under the control of a Minister. A small beginning has been made in extending technical education and fostering new or nascent industries. The supervision of the Central Government over industrial affairs still continues. The responsibility for general legislation regarding the conditions of labour in factories and mines and Trades Unions rests with the Central Government.

It is in the field of agriculture that the provinces have absolute control, though their record of work is far from satisfactory. In Bengal, the United Provinces, and Bihar and Orissa there has been no lack of official and non-official endeavour to reform the tenancy laws, but not much has been accomplished, and the grievance of the tenants still continues to supply fertile soil for political propaganda.

The real achievement lies in the silent, noble welfare-work of the co-operative societies, whose number, membership, and capital grow steadily. The co-operative societies' constructive work consists in the encouragement of thrift by collecting small shares, receiving deposits, and inducing members to make compulsory contributions for special purposes.

"It is now twenty-three years," says the latest report of the Director of Public Information, Government of India, "since the co-operative movement was started in India, and its record has been one of uninterrupted progress, the total number of co-operative societies having risen to well over 70,000."[1]

The same authority shows how the movement has its own individual features in each province. In Madras cultivators have formed societies to enable them to hold up their crops for a favourable market, and the co-operative movement is spreading among the depressed classes. In Bombay implement societies hire and maintain expensive

[1] *India in 1927–28*, p. 376.

agricultural machinery. In Assam the Department of Agriculture has been amalgamated with the co-operative society. In Bengal money-lenders have taken to investing money in the co-operative societies. In Bihar and Orissa a society has been formed to undertake farming on a large scale. In the Punjab much useful work has been done by way of the consolidation of holdings. The great work done by the co-operative societies and the vast vista of useful service which lies before them are clear to those who have glanced over the pages of the official reports of various provinces. It is gratifying that all classes, whatever their political faith, have appreciated the genuine service rendered by the movement. The Councils and Ministers in future will devote more attention to this movement, which can bring lasting happiness to the poor millions in the villages.

CHAPTER VIII

PARTIES

AFTER the General Election of 1926 there came into existence five parties in the Assembly, besides the nominated and Government group.

(1) The Swaraj Party has forty members, with Pundit Motilal Nehru and Mr S. Srinivasa Iyengar as its leaders.

(2) The Nationalist Party consists of twenty members, with Pundit Madan Mohan Malaviya and Mr M. R. Jayakar as its leaders.

(3) The Muslim Central Party, which consists of seventeen members, has no outstanding leader, and consists of many non-party men. The power in this party is Dr Suhrawardy of Bengal, once a prominent lieutenant of the late Mr C. R. Das, and Deputy Mayor of the Calcutta Corporation. The leader of this party, however, is Sir Zulfikar Ali Khan.

(4) The Independent Party consists of sixteen members, with Mr M. A. Jinnah as its leader.

(5) The Europeans, who are ten in number, have Sir Darcy Lindsay as their leader. Their party includes such an able, independent, and influential man as Sir Victor Sassoon, who is noted for his radical views and real sympathy for Indian aspirations.

The nominated members, who are forty-one in number, consist of twenty-six officials and fifteen others.

The elections of 1926 were fought clearly on national *versus* communal lines. Pundit Madan Mohan Malaviya and Lala Lajpat Rai fought Pundit Motilal Nehru and Mr Srinivasa Iyengar, on behalf of the Hindu Sabha against the Congress and its pro-Muslim Nationalism. Mr Srinivasa Iyengar, who is a very energetic politician and capable of organizing his forces, captured a large number of seats in South India. Pundit Motilal Nehru, who has the special gift of riding roughshod over the feelings of his friends and opponents, and who is ageing fast, met with what he himself mournfully described as "a veritable rout." Every Hindu Congressman in the United Provinces was defeated in a contested election, excepting the present writer, who was far from being a henchman of the Pundit, and whose victory was wholly due to his personal influence with his electorate and his work in the Legislature and the country outside. Pundit Motilal Nehru himself would have lost his seat had not Pundit Madan Mohan Malaviya with his usual generosity given him an uncontested seat.

The success of the Hindu Maha Sabha made a profound impression on the Congress leader, who practically accepted the Hindu position, and surrendered to the Maha Sabha by producing what is called the "Nehru Report" and repudiating the demands of moderate Mussulmans like Mr Mohammed Ali Jinnah.

In the Assembly the leadership passed in effect from the hands of the Congress Pundit to the Maha Sabha Pundit. The two parties, however, while adopting an identical attitude toward the Government, chose to sit in separate blocks.

The Swarajists abandoned their old policy of opposing the present constitution in season and out of season, except when Pundit Madan Mohan Malaviya gave them the lead to that effect. They also ceased to question the supremacy of the British Parliament. Their leader even went the length of raising a technical objection in the Simla Session of the Assembly in 1927, when the Government introduced the Public Safety Bill, which was directed against the propaganda of English and other alien communists, who were creating unrest in industrial areas, on the ground that the Assembly was a body subordinate to the British Parliament, which should initiate legislation in the matter. However absurd the objection might have been, its undoubted value lay in the fact that the leader of the intransigent Swarajists recognized British overlordship, which he and his followers had hitherto questioned.

The only distinction between the Swaraj Party and the other parties in the Assembly lay in their exhibition of bad manners in persisting in their meaningless boycott of the Viceregal Lodge functions in Delhi-Simla and the Government House functions in the provinces after their open co-operation on the floor of the Legislature. This ban has been resented by the sensible members of the party, who had it lifted in 1928 or earlier. The Indian National Congress, which was dragging the country into what his Excellency Lord Irwin described as the "morass" of independence, reimposed the ban at its Calcutta session in December 1928, which has been observed since by most, though not all, of the members of that party in the Central Legislature.

The anomaly of the members of the Central Legislature boycotting the Viceroy, who is the King's representative, is being recognized by those who understand the implications of their oath of allegiance to the King, his heirs and successors. The social boycott is resented by the rank and file as a violation of the oath and bordering almost on perjury. Its leader, however, retains this ugly distinction from other parties to prop up his tottering leadership.

This attitude of social boycott apart, the Swaraj Party have ceased to talk of obstruction. When the present writer moved in the Assembly the rejection of the Finance Bill in 1927 on the ground of grievances before supplies Pundit Motilal Nehru did not support the motion or vote for it, even though Pundit Madan Mohan Malaviya, whom he had denounced during the 1926 elections as a reactionary, spoke and voted for it, his whole party loyally standing by him.

The Swarajist leader has, after no small experience, inwardly recognized the futility of tall talk and meaningless obstruction, though he still outwardly persists for popularity's sake in haranguing on "revolution" and "reviving non-co-operation." The truth is that he believes in neither, and is anxious to get out of the mess he has made of Congress politics with some credit to himself.

The Swaraj Party, because of the unsettled condition of its leader's mind, owing to the slave mentality of his following—over whom his colleague Mr S. Srinivasa Iyengar, the deputy leader, thanks to his sincerity and joviality, exercises a much larger influence, both in the Legislatures and out in the country—is an unstable item in Indian politics. It is capable of going to extremes, such as the boycott of the Legislatures, which alone, the radicals among them think, can save it from internal disintegration and inept leadership. A return to the Legislatures with the slogan of obstruction may be attempted, but it has been discredited by its preachers themselves, who never consistently attempted to put it into operation.

Whatever the future of the All-India Swaraj Party may be, so far as the provinces are concerned, if official reports [1] can be relied upon, they have been in the past the most organized and also the most efficient.

The parties have varied in various provinces. In some provinces they have shown a tendency toward communalism or racialism, more than toward nationalism.

"Religious or ecclesiastical differences," says Bryce,

> have given birth to them [parties] as in England and Scotland in the seventeenth century, or racial divisions, or loyalty to

[1] Reports of the working of the Reformed Constitution, 1927.

> a dynasty. . . . Even attachment to a particular leader who has gathered followers round him may keep them together long after he has passed away. A party may in its beginnings be built on any foundation—wood or stubble as well as rock—for it is not the origin that matters so much as the forces, which, once created, a party can enlist. However, in more recent days, and especially in countries enjoying representative government, the normal source is found in the emergence of some type of political doctrine, some specific practical issue which divides the citizens, some taking one side, some another.[1]

The Brahmin and Non-Brahmin Parties in South India and the Hindu and Muslim Parties in Upper India are based on religious or caste differences and resemble the parties in England of the seventeenth century. These differences will continue to exist for several years. The exercise of responsible government in the provinces will slowly wear them down and enable the units composing them to think nationally. Attachment to a particular leader like C. R. Das in Bengal held together the Swaraj Party, which broke up after his death. The Mahratta Nationalists grouped themselves into a separate party under the label "Responsivists," whose slogan was responsive co-operation—a phrase used by Tilak at the Amritsar Congress. The Mahrattas repudiated the leadership of Mr Das's secretary, Pundit Motilal Nehru of Allahabad, who had neither the vision nor the ability of "the Tilak of Bengal," as they loved to call C. R. Das.

The Swaraj Party itself has been held together by the emergence of the ideal of *Swaraj*, though in the Provincial as in the Central Legislature it shows signs of disruption, as in the interpretation of the doctrine of *Swaraj* a difference of opinion has arisen, one school treating it as Dominion Home Rule and another as sovereign independence.

The political parties in India are in embryo. They will

[1] *Modern Democracies*, by Viscount Bryce, vol. i, p. 126.

be reshaped with the change of circumstances and the progress of responsible government. To cast the horoscope of the political parties of the self-governing India of the future may be fascinating. The political astrologer will say that the popular Radical of to-day, swept off his feet by anti-British frenzy, will be the worst Tory of a self-governing India. We are, however, concerned not with the future, which we do not know, but with the present, which we understand.

The parties which first emerged in the country were divided on the issue of reforms. One section decided to work them. Another decided to boycott them. If both had decided to try their strength within the Legislatures the reforms would have thriven on their dissensions. But as the boycotting parties were revolutionary the chance of developing constitutional parties was for the time lost. When they entered the Legislatures after three years' boycott it was after the wrecking of the opposing parties, which had supported the Government with a view to defeating their movements.

The Madras Presidency

In the Madras Presidency during the first Council the Non-Brahmin Party was easily the first in organization. It was a reform party, founded by Dr T. M. Nair, who was once a staunch Nationalist.

Had Dr Nair been alive when the reforms were inaugurated he would have saved the Non-Brahmin Party from sinking into the abyss of communalism. It was one of the tragedies of public life in Madras that this giant should have died at a time when his leadership was most needed.

The Non-Brahmin Party decided to work the reforms. Its chief opponents had boycotted the Council. Since the advent of the Swaraj Party as a separate unit, and particularly since its policy of Council entry was accepted by the Congress, it succeeded in capturing many non-Brahmin seats.

Both the Congress and the Non-Brahmin Parties practised the general method of keeping themselves in touch with the constituencies by frequent conferences at important centres. The Congress Party has a network of organizations throughout the Presidency, which it has divided for convenience sake into linguistic divisions, such as Tamil, Telegu, Kanarese, and Malabar. The Non-Brahmin Party, which was racial, excluded the Brahmins. The Congress Party, which was led by Mr S. Srinivasa Iyengar, included the non-Brahmins.

According to the official report, its "superior organization" led many non-Brahmins to join that party.[1] Partly the superior organization and partly the personal magnetism of Mr S. Srinivasa Iyengar, who, unlike his Allahabad colleague, does not squander personal friendship, are responsible for his weaning many non-Brahmins from following a policy of communal fanfaronade.

Whatever the future of the Congress Party in Madras may be, the nationalism of the Congress has percolated to the ranks of the non-Brahmins. It must at the same time be admitted that the communalism of the non-Brahmin movement has also shown a tendency to infect the Congress ranks. Such action and reaction is inevitable in politics.

A new force has been let loose in the Congress—the Independence movement. This is calculated to cause a cleavage in the Congress ranks, because Madras is the one province in India which is a sincere believer in the British connexion. The drift of most national movements is to the left. It is not unlikely that this drift may carry a section of the Madras Swarajists with it. The cleavage is inevitable, as the tendency evinced by the other section is toward a more moderate policy.

[1] Reports of the working of the Reformed Constitution, 1927.

So far as the Council parties are concerned, their political goal is Home Rule within the Empire. The Councils show the tendencies natural in all Parliaments of opposition for opposition's sake. This was revealed not only by the Swaraj Party, but also by the dispossessed Non-Brahmin Party, which opposed the Independent Ministry with "acrimony and persistence," as the official report has it.[1] It is noteworthy that the one-time professed Swarajist policy of "uniform, consistent, and continuous obstruction within the Councils" has practically never been pursued in Madras. This may be due to the fact that the Swarajists are in close touch with their constituencies, which do not believe in barren obstruction.

One of the most important facts to reckon with in future in the Madras Presidency is the growth of a class sentiment among labour units. Labour is suspicious and unwilling to get entangled with any particular party. Both the Swarajist and Justice Parties are flirting with labour: the former press for affiliation with the Congress, the latter advocate the formation of a separate Labour entity. It is impossible to say at present what the developments will be, but the position is interesting. "The Labour unions have shown no sign of any desire to attach Labour to the wheels of the Congress or any other chariot," says the official report. This is a wise policy. Labour must exploit both the parties instead of being exploited.[2]

The future of party contests in Madras is difficult to adumbrate with any precision. One broad fact, however, emerges from the conflict of parties to-day. The activities of the Justice Party, which has its organization in the South Indian Liberal Federation, have been increasing. Its programme includes increased control of religious endowments and development of industries. The official report says

[1] Reports of the working of the Reformed Constitution, 1927.

[2] The Simon Commission are expected to give their special attention to Labour and the creation of special Labour constituencies.

that this party has achieved a definite degree of progress toward these objects. But their achievement has not, at any rate, been appreciated by their constituents, which accounts for a split in their own camp and the dwindling of their numbers. If the Congress decides to plough the sands of non-co-operation and chase the will-o'-the-wisp of independence, and, finally, to boycott the Legislatures, the Justice Party will not hesitate to profit by the unwisdom of its opponents, and establish a position for itself which would remain unassailable for some years.

The Punjab

In the Punjab, of the sixty-nine elected seats about thirty-seven were held by members of the Unionist, or Rural, Party. The majority of them were Muslims and the minority Hindus or Sikhs. The minority party was prepared to co-operate with the opposing community on questions involving a clash of rural with urban interests. Of the remaining elected seats, twelve were held by Swarajists, three by Khalifatists, nine by Sikhs, who were nominees of the Shromani Gurdwara Parbandhak Committee, and the balance was held by members who called themselves Independents. The Swarajists have not been effective in the Punjab, and may not be for some time to come. The parties in the Punjab really divide themselves communally as Sikhs, Hindus, and Muslims. The Swarajists, however, have succeeded now and again in securing the support of some Hindu and Sikh members, not in the pursuit of their policy of obstruction, which was not attempted in the Punjab, but to fan the feeling of interested members in regard to the Governor's selection of Ministers. This was based more on personal and less on political grounds.

The extreme tactics of the Swarajists found little support or sympathy in the Council itself, where the other minority parties feared an attitude of uncompromising hostility might result in forcing the Government into the arms of the Mohammedan rural party. Their influence in the Council had a salutary effect on the Swarajists, who, in the language of the official report, were "at first a destructive, and later a more discriminating critic." Before the Council was dissolved the policy of non-co-operation was as dead as a door-nail.

In March 1926 eight members of the Swaraj Party, acting on instructions from headquarters, 'walked out' as a protest against the failure of the Government to grant a further instalment of reforms, but these pedestrian politics covered the Swarajists with ridicule, as their leader himself bravely confessed in the Subjects Committee of the Gauhati Congress.

The Khalifatist coterie was a negligible factor in the Punjab Councils, for the reason that its leading lights, like Dr Kitchlew of Amritsar, did not believe in Council entry. They believed in revolutionary, and not Parliamentary, action.

The Sikh Party leaders were effective debaters, but the rank and file were mere voting automatons.

The very few good speakers were naturally the better educated, and therefore the more moderate members of the group, says the official review.

Generally speaking, the Unionist majority were Ministerialists. They expected the Ministers to uphold rural interests.

> The majority of the members of the party were men of the yeoman type, on the whole conservative in their general outlook, shrewd in practical matters, loyal by tradition and instinct to Government, proud of the martial traditions of their tribes, and consistent in their efforts to promote the interests of the small yeomen and land-owners' class, if necessary at the expense of the townsmen.

It may be said of the second reformed Council, as of the first, that it represented the more moderate current of public opinion in the province, and that its relations with the Executive were harmonious. Though occasionally inspired by the idea of placating advanced public opinion, as, for instance, in a resolution which was carried by a large majority recommending the release from gaol of the Khalifatist, Zafar Ali Khan, it has approached most questions in what the official report calls "a spirit of moderation," tempered, perhaps, by a disposition toward criticism of Government measures. For example, says the report of the Punjab Government, on the enhancement of canal charges the general feeling of the Rural Party was one of steady opposition, but the tone of the speech was always moderate. A non-official resolution urging the removal of the statue of Lord Lawrence at Lahore—the soldier-statesman who preferred the sword to the pen—was defeated by a substantial majority after a lively but by no means heated debate. The proposals of the Muddiman Committee were condemned as inadequate after a dull debate in March 1925, but political theories as a rule are a secondary consideration with the majority of Punjab representatives, who believe in practical measures.

The United Provinces

Parties on modern lines made their appearance in the United Provinces Council in 1923. The preceding Councils, which the non-co-operators had boycotted, had contained a group of Liberals who on most questions voted together, but they lacked discipline and a clear-cut programme. When the Swarajists entered the Council they were thirty in number. Their organization, says the official report, "gave them an importance above their numerical strength." The power of the Swarajists waned and their number dwindled in the third Council owing to the split in the Congress camp, thanks to the Hindu Maha Sabha's war on the Congress. Owing to the decrease in their number and the impatience of the majority in the Council with their extreme tactics the Swarajists gave up their programme of direct action and behaved like sober men.

A new party was formed, called the Nationalist Party, consisting of twenty-eight members belonging to the Hindu Sabha and the National Liberal Federation. Some landlords have also joined them. "It is a purely Hindu party," says the official report. No Muslims have joined it. Though the Nationalist Party have not chosen to unite with the Swarajists and form a reunited Nationalist Party, their policy and aims are identical. Their immediate goal is provincial autonomy, the grant of which will satisfy them.

Both the Swarajists and Nationalists have invariably combined in speeches and votes alike in their severe attacks on the Reserved side of the Government. "Towards Ministers the attitude of the Nationalists is mainly determined by personal considerations," says the official report.

The Swaraj Party can be compared to Radicals; the Nationalists to Liberals; and the landlords to Conservatives. Numerically the largest, and first in point of opulence, the landlords have shown no capacity for organization.

The Muslims form a party by themselves, and have shown a tendency to co-operate with the Government on essential matters. In this the Government also manage to secure the co-operation of some Hindus, about fifteen in number.

"Communal feeling was strong though usually latent in the second Council," says the official report. It is burrowing underground in the present Legislature. For tactical reasons the Nationalists and Swarajists have refrained from bringing forward any motion which would be regarded by the Mohammedans as a direct challenge. Curiously enough, an attack by a member of one community on a Minister or Member of the Executive Council belonging to the other community is viewed with suspicion by the criticized official's co-religionists, who generally rally to his support.

Developments on party lines, which have been rapid, will

prove stable with the grant of autonomy. The Swarajists, who are still opposed to the formation of Ministries, will abandon this policy the moment complete responsibility is introduced. The Government do not take seriously the Swarajist professions of non-acceptance of office. The Swarajists serve on committees. One of the Swarajists is the Deputy President of the Council. The Government's reading of Pundit Govind Ballabh Pant, the leader of the Swarajist Party, with twenty-two followers, is interesting:

> He was formerly a Liberal, and is still so by temperament and conviction. He has never professed to take seriously the cult of the *charka*[1] (spinning-wheel), and probably regrets the refusal of the Congress to abandon completely the non-co-operation programme. His tactical skill is considerable, and was responsible for his party's decisive influence in the debates of the Agra Tenancy Bill. Of late, however, his position has been somewhat weakened by the advent of Mr Chintamani (the Liberal leader and ex-Minister), whose vehement utterances appeal strongly to some of the Swarajists.

BENGAL

In Bengal Das held together the Hindus and Muslims and successfully practised obstruction. He was the only Indian leader who carried out his pledge of suspending dyarchy by a policy of uniform, continuous, consistent obstruction. Dyarchy was suspended in Bengal during his lifetime. The Swaraj Party had a powerful organ, *Forward*, a daily paper founded by Das, with a large circulation. Its editors often go to prison for their anti-British articles. The *Forward* itself came to grief because of its extremism; and its publication had to be suspended. Its place has been taken by an equally powerful organ, *Liberty*.

The Independent Party—though the name is a paradox,

[1] One of Gandhi's strongest objections was to the wearing by Indians of cloth manufactured outside India; hence "the cult of the *charka*." Gandhi's object was to revive India's industries.

the Independents being hardly the material out of which a party could be made—in important moves against the Government, and especially in the matter of upsetting Ministries, invariably joined hands with the great Das, who could thus usually command 66 votes in a house of 140. After the passing away of Das the Muslims left the Swaraj Party in large numbers and formed a Mohammedan group. This disintegration was due to the fact that the leadership of the party passed into the hands of a lesser man in Allahabad, who had neither a cool head nor a restrained tongue, nor yet the courage of his convictions. The Muslims had anticipated that the Swarajists would prove to be Hindus first and Nationalists afterward when the British Commission of Inquiry should be appointed. The Nehru Report not only repudiated the Muslim claims, but also the Hindu-Muslim pact of Das.

Besides the Swaraj Party, who are organized and disciplined, the only other organized party is the European and Anglo-Indian group. They have a common aim and object, a leader whom they respect, a party whip, and a powerful Press in the *Englishman* and *Statesman*. The European group has been a tower of strength to the Government, who could always rely on them as they could rely on the nominated members.

The so-called obstructionists in Bengal will settle down to work the reforms when Bengal is given provincial autonomy. There is a strong group among the Swarajists which feels that the moment autonomy is granted in Bengal, whatever their policy in the Central Government might be, they cannot honestly avoid accepting office. Mr Sen Gupta, a talented and forceful personality, who has succeeded Mr C. R. Das in provincial leadership, might legitimately aspire to be the Prime Minister of the Swarajist Government in Bengal, with Subosh Chandra Bose, formerly of the Indian Civil Service, and now the leader of the Congress left wing, as Home Secretary.

There is a large section of conservative landlords in Bengal who are not properly organized, and who have been made to feel that they should organize themselves.

The above cursory survey of the working of parties in some of the leading provinces will suffice for our present purpose.

Political philosophers have always deplored party systems. They say that once parties uprear themselves good causes cannot thrive.

"I can never extract from Mr Goldwin Smith, with all his mastery of history and political acumen," writes Bryce, "any answer to the question how representative government could be carried on without them." [1]

Parties in India are no doubt imperfect. The leaders are apt to look upon them as their private appendage. Parties may have shown a tendency, owing to incompetent leadership—especially among the Swarajists—to degenerate into an odious kind of tyranny. But the leaders are only amateurs. With the growth of traditions and responsible government parties would develop necessary coherence and principles.

Some tender souls despaired, especially during the 1926 elections, owing to the personal rivalries of two leaders of the Congress and the Hindu Sabha, as to whether India was fit for *Swaraj*.

Bryce says he knew of a Scottish constituency in which a party had been similarly divided on account of the personal dissensions of the leaders more than of political differences, "but each held together and during a long series of years tried to carry a candidate of its own, merely because each desired to be the ruling force in the town." [2] This was the case in Allahabad between the two Pundits, Malaviya and Motilal. They appear to have made up their differences for the present. The Swarajist leader's squabbles with his

[1] *Modern Democracies*, vol. i, p. 138. [2] *Ibid.*, p. 127.

contemporaries remind one of the happenings in the Italian republics in the Middle Ages, where personal animosities of rival leaders used to be the basis for political factions.

Such dissensions are not altogether unknown to modern countries. England witnessed a similar occurrence when the differences of Mr Asquith and Mr Lloyd George tore the Liberal Party asunder.[1]

Lively quarrels between political leaders only indicate that India is experiencing the birth-pangs of freedom.

[1] That the bitterness which accrued from this painful personal controversy had not died was revealed by a recent speech made by one of the greatest Liberals living, Earl Grey, who frankly confessed his and his friends' inability to work with Mr Lloyd George.

CHAPTER IX

THE ELECTORATES

THE Montagu-Chelmsford Report laid down some broad principles, which were worked out in detail by a committee presided over by Lord Southborough, known as the Franchise and Functions Committee. This Committee toured throughout the country from November 1918 till March 1919, and made its recommendations in regard to the electorate under the reforms.

Principal among the qualifications which the Committee recommended were a property qualification and residence within the constituency. No uniform property qualification was fixed for the various provinces or, for that matter, for the various electoral areas in one and the same province, with the result that the electoral qualifications differed between one area and another in the same province, and between one province and another. There was also much disparity between the enfranchized proportions and the actual populations of the various provinces. Moreover, an unequal distribution of representation between the rural and urban populations could not be avoided.

The other recommendations of the Franchise Committee related to the enfranchisement of all retired and pensioned officers of the Indian Army, whether of commissioned or non-commissioned rank; the denial of franchise to women, to the subjects of foreign states, and to persons under twenty-one and those of unsound mind and guilty of offences involving moral turpitude; the grant of votes to subjects of Indian States; and the withdrawal of the Governor's right to nullify the election of a candidate as contrary to public interest.

The Franchise Committee further recommended that the existing system of indirect election should be replaced by direct election in the case of the Provincial Legislatures, but retained in regard to both Houses of the Central Legislature.

As regards separate representation of communities, the Committee recommended its retention so far as the Mussulmans were concerned and its extension to the Sikhs in the Punjab, the Indian Christians in Madras, the Europeans in Bombay, Bengal and Madras, the United Provinces and Bihar and Orissa, and the Anglo-Indians in Madras and Bengal, but not to the Mahrattas of Bombay and the non-Brahmins in Madras.

The Government of India dissented from some of the recommendations of the Franchise Committee. They objected to subjects of Indian States as electors or candidates for Councils, and to franchise qualifications other than those based on property.

Had the recommendations of the Government of India been accepted the franchise would have been so varied as to result in a meagre enlargement of the Punjab electorate and a vast expansion of the Madras electorate. They were for reducing by about one-third the large electorates proposed by the Franchise Committee for Bengal, the United Provinces, and Assam. They thought the proposed provision for representation of the depressed classes was insufficient, and disapproved of the proposed university constituencies.

While endorsing the Franchise Committee's recommendations regarding communal electorates the Government of India considered that the strength of Muslim representation in Bengal was inadequate. The Government did not approve of the Committee's rejection of the non-Brahmin claims to separate representation.

While accepting as a temporary measure the Committee's recommendation of indirect elections to Assembly the Government of India opined that the elections for the Council of States should at least be direct.

The Joint Committee of the British Parliament heard the Indian representatives, who disapproved of some important recommendations of the Franchise Committee, while agreeing with the Government of India that the elections to the Council of State should be direct. The Joint Committee further agreed with the Indian leaders that the election of the non-official members to the Legislative Assembly should also be direct, and not through the Provincial Councils. The Joint Committee modified some of the recommendations of the Franchise Committee, and made more acceptable suggestions, many of which were incorporated in the Government of India Act and rules made thereunder.

The first elections to the new Legislatures took place in November 1920. The non-co-operators, under the leadership of Mahatma Gandhi and the Indian National Congress, preached boycott of the elections and the reforms. Polling-booths in various provinces were picketed. Neither candidates nor voters, however, were lacking, though there is no gainsaying the fact that the non-co-operators succeeded in dissuading several of the newly enfranchized people from exercising their votes. This was not much of an achievement, as the task of taking the voters to the polls is difficult even in advanced countries. In England, where democratic institutions have reached a high degree of perfection, and where the electorate is far from indifferent, parties and politicians have invariably grumbled after every General Election at the lethargy of the electors.

The non-co-operators did not succeed in regard to their attempt to defeat the elections by persuading candidates not to stand. Out of 637 elections only six were not held owing to the absence of a candidate.

The greatest achievement of the non-co-operators was in Bombay City, where the influence and the presence of Mahatma Gandhi was no mean factor to reckon with. Only 8 per cent. of the enfranchized section recorded their votes in Bombay City. In the Madras Presidency, where the non-co-operators exercised less influence, as many as 70 per cent. of votes were recorded in some of the urban constituencies. In the Punjab, notwithstanding the bitterness in the minds of the people owing to unfortunate events, the voting in general constituencies was as high as 32 per cent., and in the rural constituencies 36 per cent. In the United Provinces, where Liberalism offered the stoutest resistance to the non-co-operators during the election—and stubborn support to the Government in the three subsequent years in the maintenance of law and order, even though it involved the imprisonment of hundreds of Congressmen—the voting in Lucknow and some other centres was as high as 60 per cent., while the average in other contested constituencies could be estimated at 33 per cent. According to the official estimates, the voting in the first elections for the Provincial Councils averaged for the whole country at between 20 and 30 per cent., for the Legislative Assembly at 20 per cent., and for the Council of State at 40 per cent.

Bearing in mind the unprecedented enthusiasm aroused by the non-co-operation movement, the above figures prove that even at a time when the boycott propaganda was at its fiercest the electorate attached appreciable value to their power to vote.

The boycott was called off by the Congress during the 1923 elections in deference to Das and the Swaraj Party, who wanted to enter the Councils on the distinct understanding that neither the Congress machinery nor its funds were to be used for that purpose. There was a straight fight in many places between the Swarajists and the Liberals and other co-operators. The former denounced the latter for having allied themselves with an "alien Government" to defeat and discredit the Freedom-for-India movement by imprisoning the venerable leaders of the Congress and their numerous followers. The latter retorted that law and order must be maintained and the King's Government carried on. The Liberals were wiped out. Even veterans like Sir Surendranath Bannerjee were defeated. The enthusiasm aroused by the elections was unprecedented. "The fight," says an official report, "was cleanly conducted." This is a glowing testimony to the fair methods of the two great veterans, now no longer with us, the late Deshabhandu C. R. Das and Sir Surendranath Bannerjee.

On entering the Councils the first inquiry of the triumphant Swarajists was, like the celebrated question at the Mormon wedding, "How many of her are there?" Actually there was only one elected non-official Liberal in the Assembly of 1923. He too was defeated in the 1926 elections. But again there came from the United Provinces one Liberal. Their future, however, is bright, owing to their diplomatic manipulation of the Swarajist leader, whom they assisted in producing a report on the lines laid down by the Liberal leaders in their presidential speeches in their annual conferences.

The elections of 1923 showed that in contested constituencies the number of votes recorded was nearly double those in the previous elections. Out of 800,000 votes in contested elections more than 350,000 were recorded for the Legislative Assembly. For the Provincial Councils, in contested constituencies, between 40 and 50 per cent. of votes were recorded.

The elections of 1925 to the Council of State disclosed that its constituencies were still Conservative. The Swaraj Party made a strenuous attempt to capture some of the seats, but they could only return nine out of a total of thirty-three members.

The General Elections of 1926 for the Legislative Assembly and the Provincial Councils witnessed the rout of the Congress in Upper India and the triumph of the Communalists, who had rallied under the banner of the

Hindu Maha Sabha. This was partly due to the lack of drive in the Congress leadership, which was played out, and the lack of character of the Congress Party, which was being eaten up by internal jealousy and petty feuds. A powerful leader with infinite patience and capacity for sacrifice was able to hold together men of various temperaments and outlook. His tact and his genius for compromise, yielding on non-essentials to please the *amour propre* of his prominent followers, while sticking to his own general policy, gave C. R. Das unique power and opportunity. Mr Das was not oppressed by the vanity of a mediocre politician of Allahabad who succeeded him in the All-India leadership, and who got into endless trouble with his colleagues because he had not the ordinary ability of a leader to merge his ego in the greater ego of his own party and the still greater ego of his own country.

In South India, and especially in the Madras Presidency, the non-Brahmin party, which had become a communal caucus, was easily routed by the Congress leader, whose energy and diplomacy confounded his opponents. The driving-power of the Swarajist leader of South India, his enthusiasm for the cause, and his capacity for complete self-effacement made Mr Srinivasa Iyengar the idol of the public. But for his personality, to which the Swarajist successes in the South must be wholly attributed, the strength of the Congress Party would have considerably decreased in the Legislative Assembly. Despite all this, the Swarajists lost both in numbers and prestige in the Legislative Assembly and the Provincial Councils. To avoid the Swarajists being 'dished' at the next elections their leader surrendered the Congress programme and abandoned the old Nationalist policy which believed in healthy compromises with Muslims with a view to creating confidence in an important minority, without which all national endeavours must end in fiasco. The spirit which animated the old Congress and gave India what was known as "the Lucknow Pact," the strength behind which compelled the Government to incorporate it in the 1919 scheme of the reforms, was banished from the Congress owing to the lack of faith and lack of courage of its leader, who could not forget the heavy casualties of the 1916 elections. A constitutional scheme of reforms which was acceptable to the Hindu Maha Sabha was produced by the Congress leaders with the help of the Liberals, to the disgust of the Muslims and the Sikhs, who openly rebelled against it. This incident shows that organized communalism can confuse and overwhelm professing nationalism.

It was becoming clear that the power of the electorate was being felt by the leaders. Its communalism became contagious. Separate electorates cannot be the nurseries of nationalism. The Congress became tainted with communalism because it believed in Council entry and had to pander to the prejudices of the electors. The Muslims in the Congress dwindled from a few hundreds to less than a score of members. The Congress had asked the voters not to exercise their new rights. When the first period of ten years' reforms was about to expire the very Congress felt compelled to bow to the electorate, which was communal. The parties and their leaders could not therefore afford to take up a purely nationalist attitude. This is true alike of Hindus and Muslims.

The awakening of the electorate was real. Their interest in the administration of the country and in the work of the Legislatures was increasing.

In the United Provinces, which has a population of 45,375,000, the electorate in 1920 was over a million. In 1923 half a million more electors, and by 1926 another 100,000, were added to the rolls, making a percentage of 3·53 to the total population. The percentage of votes polled in 1920 was 33. It rose to 41·36 in 1923 and 49·32 in 1926. In 1920 the total number of votes recorded was 333,000. In 1923 the total number was 510,511. And in 1926 it rose to

732,155, many more than double the number of votes polled in the first General Election under the Montagu reforms.

In the Punjab, which has a total population of a little over 20,500,000, the number of those who were enfranchized was 702,748, or 3·3 per cent. At the General Election of 1923 the percentage of votes polled varied from 84 in the case of the university constituency to 38 in the case of the ten Sikh constituencies.

In Bengal in 1923 the number of voters was 1,044,116, or 2·1 per cent. of the population. Of these 34·8 per cent. recorded their votes in 1923. The number of electors in 1926 was 1,184,804, or 2·4 per cent. of the population. Of these 33·4 per cent. voted in 1926.

In the Madras Presidency in 1920 3 per cent. of the total population were enfranchized, and 24 per cent. of the registered voters exercised the right to vote. In 1923 3·13 per cent. were registered as voters, and 36·26 per cent. of the voters went to the polls. In 1926 3·36 were enfranchized, and 48 per cent. of them exercised their franchise. In 1923 women were entitled to vote. In 1926 women were allowed to stand as candidates, though the two who stood were defeated.

In the Bombay Presidency in 1923 the percentage of voters to total population was 4·03 for the Legislative Council and ·98 for the Legislative Assembly. The percentage of votes recorded to the total number of voters on the electoral roll is estimated at 69·84 for the Provincial Council and 70·97 for the Assembly.

In the Central Provinces and Berar the percentage of male electors who voted in the General Election of 1923 in contested general constituencies to the total number of registered voters was 57·4.

In Bihar and Orissa, during the 1923 election, the polling was far heavier than in 1920, averaging 52 per cent. for the Provincial Council. In 1926 the percentage of actual voters rose to 60 in the contested constituencies.

In Assam, in contested constituencies, 25 per cent. went to the polls in 1920, 42 per cent. in 1923; and 43·5 per cent. in 1926. At the last General Election the highest proportion of polling was in the Mohammedan constituency of South Sylhet, 71 per cent.; and the next in the Sylhet Sadr Non-Mohammedan constituency, 66·11 per cent.

It must be remembered that greater enthusiasm cannot be created for a Legislature which has no power to enforce the will of the people. With the grant of autonomy, the growth of education among people, and the realization of their powers arising from the dependence of the parties on the voters the electorates may be expected to take as real an interest in the administration as the electors in any other part of the civilized world.

Limited as the powers of the present Legislatures are, the interest evinced by the constituencies and the general public in the work of the Councils is striking. The following observations of the Madras Government are noteworthy:

> The work of the Council is followed closely by the literate and particularly by the English-educated population. The Press gives much space to reports of debates, and its correspondence columns frequently contain letters demanding or suggesting or complaining of action by the Council. Members of the Council on occasions contribute to such correspondence, thus recognizing that by this means they may secure a wider hearing. The Visitors' Gallery is well patronized, and indeed is uncomfortably crowded during important debates, such as that on the University Bill, or the Religious Endowments Bill. Such measures produce a large crop of newspaper leaders. Important resolutions, *e.g.*, that in favour of the enfranchisement of women, those for adjournment of the House, the more sensational Budget motions, arouse much interest. The interest is keener in Madras than in the country districts, but even there meetings to support or condemn decisions of the legislative body are not unknown, and the resolutions of such meetings are on occasions forwarded to Government.

CHAPTER X

THE PUBLIC SERVICES

Lord Meston (retired I.C.S.) quotes with approval the Abbé Reynal, who declared that had the Portuguese not rounded the Cape of Good Hope and discovered India the torch of Liberty in Europe would have been extinguished by the Turks, and Islam would have dominated the world.[1] The French philosopher-historian has been proved right by the testimony of the twentieth century. Muslim thinkers hold that had the flag of Indian nationalism not been seized by European hands the Turks would not have been beaten back to their Asiatic homelands. The conquest of India laid the foundations of the success of the European movement against Turkey and of the British Commonwealth.

Had the Empire of the Moghuls not sunk under the vices of bad internal administration and the excesses of Aurangzeb's fanaticism, the revulsion against it under Sivaji's leadership would not have assumed such gigantic proportions, and the central Government would not have fallen a prey to irretrievable demoralization. Under the circumstances nothing could be easier than the passing of the Empire of the Moghuls and the Mahrattas within the orbit of the British Commonwealth.

Had the English trodden the path of the Grand Moghul they would have marched down the steep incline, and their Empire in India would have long since become a thing of the past. Their first attempt was to study and avoid the mistakes of their predecessors.

The one insuperable obstacle in the way of the consolidation of their power was their ignorance of the

[1] *The Dominions and Dependencies of the Empire.*

vernaculars of the country, an ignorance which they overcame by the brilliant plan of educating the Hindus in English. Quite a reasonable volume can be compiled from the correspondence of the early British administrators on this subject. The prop of British rule in India has been neither the Army nor the police, but the English-educated classes who carry on the government of the country. The steel frame of the structure was not the European Services, but the English-educated classes turned out by the Indian universities. As the number of the universities and the students who passed out of them increased beyond the requirements of an earlier day the growth of middle-class unemployment became a serious problem. The educated unemployed middle classes naturally contribute to our present discontents.

Macaulay foresaw this trouble, and claimed that it would be the proudest chapter of English history. In no case could it be avoided. The choice lay between colonizing India—which was out of the question—and Europeanizing her children. True is the contention of British critics that the clamour for Indianization of the superior Services and nationalization of the administration emanates from educated classes, whose success will only mean the transfer of power from a white bureaucracy to a brown oligarchy. But the retort of the latter is equally true, that they are numerically larger than the former, have a greater stake in the country, and are not migratory birds. It is a recognition of the validity of the claim of the educated classes that resulted in the famous O'Donnell Circular.

It would be interesting to see what the official opinion is on the subject:

> More powerful still has been the general uncertainty as to what the immediate future would bring to the English administrator in India—an uncertainty aggravated by the depressing atmosphere of racial hatred which had begun to surround

even those who were devoting themselves most whole-heartedly to the interests of their adopted country. The result of all these factors was a serious shortage in suitable European candidates for the various Services. This shortage, combined with the plain desire of the Central Legislature that steps should be taken to secure an increased recruitment of Indians, induced the Government of India, with the consent of the Secretary of State, to consult local Governments on the issues involved. Accordingly a letter, which subsequently became famous as the "O'Donnell Circular," was issued at the end of May 1922. This document reviewed, and invited the opinion of the Provincial Governments upon, the various considerations involved in the question of Indianization, in order that the Government of India might consider the whole position. The letter, which had not been written for publication, was given to the world through journalistic enterprise; and at once certain sections of opinion, both in England and in India, began to accuse the Indian Government of betraying the cause of the Europeans in the Services, and of jettisoning, for political considerations, the responsibilities which Great Britain still retains for the welfare of the people of India. This agitation, together with the existing anxiety regarding the future of the Services, led Mr Lloyd George to deliver a speech early in August, in which he declared that the Civil Services of India were the steel frame of the whole structure of administration. He stated that the constitutional changes recently made in India were the result of an experiment; that he could not predict the influence which non-co-operation would exert upon the next elections; and that if there was a change in the character of the Legislature and in the purpose of those who were chosen to sit therein, the new situation would have to be taken into account. He declared that his Majesty's Government would stand to their responsibilities in India, and would take whatever steps were necessary to discharge or to enforce them. He further went on to say that he could see no period when India could dispense with the guidance and the assistance of a nucleus of the British Civil Services. The continued assistance of British Officials was, he said, necessary to bring about the discharge of Britain's great trust in India; and it was not in order to relinquish this trust, but to bring India into partnership in its discharge, that the reforms had been introduced.[1]

Say what Lloyd George may, if the goal of British rule in India is *Swaraj*, as announced by his Majesty King George on February 9, 1921, it is not right to declare, as the Welsh Prime Minister did, that he could see no period when India could dispense with the guidance of the British in the Civil Services. Another great Liberal, as Secretary of State for India, repudiated any intention of paving the way for a Parliamentary system of government in India, which, he said, " if my existence either officially or corporeally were to be prolonged twenty times longer than it is likely to be, is not at all the goal to which I could for a moment aspire."

Lord Morley was wrong. Notwithstanding his repudiation, the Indian Councils Act of 1909, which embodied what is known as the Morley-Minto reforms, was clearly paving the way for the Parliamentary system. The Montagu-Chelmsford Report shows how

> British policy in India has been steadily directed to a point at which the question of a self-governing India was bound to arise ; how impulses, at first faint, have been encouraged by education and opportunity ; how the growth quickened nine years ago, and was immeasurably accelerated by the War.

No better explanation of this immeasurable acceleration can be given than in the words of two recent authors, both of whom hold progressive if cautious views in regard to India.

> Imperial strategy before 1914 was based on the assumption that in time of hostilities India would need to be powerfully reinforced from Britain. How vastly different was our experience. The moment war was declared the Viceroy pledged the last man and the last gun in India to the service of the Crown. An immense stream of men and munitions flowed

[1] *India in 1922–23.*

from India to the various theatres of the War; a million men for service overseas, a cash contribution of a hundred millions sterling from resources which are not very large. Except for the Ghadr conspiracy in the Punjab and a momentary flicker of excitement when it was known that an attempt was to be made to land arms and ammunition from Java, the Government of India were free to pursue their Great War activities unperturbed by internal anxieties. Certainly none in India thought that thereafter India was going to stand, politically, on the ground she occupied in 1914. The last part of Lord Hardinge's Viceroyalty was devoted to an examination of the changes thought wise and prudent. Lord Chelmsford took up the question where Lord Hardinge left it. The Indian National Congress and the Moslem League adumbrated their own schemes; every one was constitution-making, and the drum-beat of self-determination raised wild hopes, unloosed soaring ambitions.[1]

Lord Morley could not have foreseen the World War and India's share in bringing it to a victorious conclusion for Britain and the Allies, but, war or no war, he should have seen, as a student of history and of human nature, the inevitable outcome of his reforms. Well might his critics say:

> Dry theorists like Lord Morley may have repudiated the idea that they were aiming at a Parliamentary system; they failed to determine what else they had in view. British policy in India has been steadily directed to a point where the question of a self-governing India was bound to arise; that it has arisen is the crowning achievement and justification of the British connexion.[2]

The spirit behind the crowning achievement was obviously not grasped by Mr Lloyd George when he insisted on the domination of the British in the Services, which was a negation of self-government. Mr Lloyd George's statement

[1] *India: the New Phase*, by Sir Stanley Reed and P. R. Cadell (published in 1928).
[2] *Ibid.*

only showed to the Indian mind that British politicians have put the War, and all the promises they made under its pressure, resolutely behind them. Colonial self-government, which is England's oft-repeated pledge to India, will have no meaning if it does not mean the approximation of the Indian Services, alike in the matter of recruitment and status, to those in the Colonies.

The criticism that the adoption of the colonial practice in regard to recruitment will reduce the efficiency of the Services is not admitted as just by the Indian politicians, but such criticism, which has always been levelled at the Colonial Services by "God's Englishmen," did not prevent the grant of self-government to the Colonies.

Keith says that the Civil Service in the Dominions is recruited from a comparatively low educational test, and then advanced by promotion, disregarding the British distinction of different educational tests according to the nature of intelligence required for the work to be accomplished.[1] The charge of a low educational test cannot be levelled against Indians. On the contrary, the complaint has been that Indians, especially the Brahmins, whose intellect is about the best in the world, have an unparalleled capacity for standing educational tests, however high. If there were no fixing of the British percentage in the Services, and educational tests were the only door of admission, India's Brahmins would swamp the Services.

According to the Indian Nationalist, there should be no fixing of percentage for the Civil Services, nor should there be simultaneous examinations in India and England. Henceforth they should be held in India only, and willing Britons aspiring to serve India, which many of them, owing to long family connexions, truly love, will do well to come to India and pass the examinations. This spirit, which inspired the O'Donnell Circular, awaits translation into actuality.

The immediate stoppage of recruitment in England is not

[1] *The Constitution, Administration, and Laws of the Empire*, by A. B. Keith.

pressed for by the Moderates, but they maintain that it is a goal toward which a rapid move must be made. Until the goal is reached they would agree to the holding of examinations in India and England. In the meantime they demand that the position of the Services must be made analogous to their position in the Colonies or Great Britain.

"Our policy," wrote the authors of the Montagu-Chelmsford Report, "is irrevocably declared, and it ought to content all sober minds. We are no longer seeking to govern a subject race by means of the Services. We are seeking to make Indian people self-governing." [1] Montagu foresaw that the change would not be agreeable to many men who had grown up in the older tradition. "It is harder to convince than to direct; to prevail in consultation than to enforce an order." [2]

To-day the Indian Civil Service dreads the political influence, whereas the politician objects to the Civil Service playing his *rôle*. He says that the Civil Service should be put beyond the pale of political influence, and demands that it should not play the politician's part. "In Australia," says Keith,

> the dread of political influence in the Civil Service has led to efforts to remove the Service in large measure from Ministerial control by conferring ample powers on Civil Service Commissions, both as regards appointment, promotion, and discipline, and the same attempt is made in the Union of South Africa. . . . In Canada, it was only in 1928 that fairly effective means were taken to bring the outside Services as well as those at Ottawa under the Civil Service Commission, and thus destroy the grave abuse of political patronage which caused numerous changes of incumbents of office on every change in the Government and destroyed the possibility of efficiency.[3]

[1] Montagu-Chelmsford Report, par. 324.
[2] *Ibid.*, par. 327.
[3] *The Constitution, Administration, and Laws of the Empire*, pp. 213, 214.

The Indian, however extreme his views may be, agrees to the grant of necessary protection which the Colonies have granted to the Services. But the Services must serve, says he; they must cease to dominate. That the Services will have much real share in shaping affairs goes without saying, but they can no longer be in the limelight; they will be relegated to the background, as in England.

The Civil Service of self-governing India should be like the Civil Service in England, without the defects of the English system. A Civil servant in Britain holds office at the pleasure of the Crown, and may be dismissed without ground, but in practice he enjoys a security of tenure without parallel in business life. This is doubtless necessary, as Keith says, in order to secure the maximum efficiency. It should not be imagined that the permanent officials have no power in Britain. The Ministers are ordinarily at their mercy. Even a man of real ability, like Mr Wedgwood Benn, is helpless in their hands. It is doubtful if even men of Mr Churchill's calibre can resist what Mr Keith calls the more subtle form of the raising of objections, supported by a wealth of knowledge and argument against which it is hard to contend.

This power of the permanent Services, while no doubt making for continuity and stability, is also responsible, in Keith's words,

> for the maintenance of abuses; the system also is marked by a vast waste of energy and of money in the duplication of work, and the obliteration of the sense of responsibility. The experience of the War showed the fatal extravagance and mismanagement in finance of Civil servants, for whom the money was provided perforce by a hapless public, while none of the tests available in business life for weeding out incompetence were applied.[1]

Thus it will be seen that even the Public Services in Britain are not filled by the infallibles.

[1] *The Constitution, Administration, and Laws of the Empire*, p. 167.

THE PUBLIC SERVICES

The object of the Indian Nationalist, which is to reduce the Civil Services in his country to the position of the same in England, may not be easy to attain. The magnitude of his task will be understood only by those who realize the power which the British attained after the battle of Plassey, and to which they have clung since. The British servants of the Company, who were merely traders, found themselves suddenly invested with the absolute powers of their predecessors. They could not overcome the grasping nature of the agencies of the Old Indian Government, which they continued to employ while steadily striving to Anglicize them.

The late Sir Valentine Chirol wrote :

> The disappearance of the old East India Company produced no radical change in the machinery or methods of Government. But the increasing complexity of Indian administration and the specialization of work in separate departments to meet the growing needs of Indian development led by degrees to excessive centralization in the Provincial and Central Government Secretariats, and these developed the usual tendency of all powerful bureaucracies to believe in their own infallibility.[1]

Pari passu with the growth in strength of this bureaucracy also grew in number what Justice Ranade called " the children of British rule."

" No nation," says Chirol,

> has been so successful as the British in ruling primitive and backward peoples who do not aspire to equality but are content as children are, but the Englishman is apt to grow impatient when those whom his tutelage has raised begin to chafe under it and demand emancipation from his leading-strings.

On the contrary, the Nationalist thinks that the British Civil servant in India has been too patient to release India from his leading-strings, and consequently has done everything in his power to create in her children healthy impatience.

[1] *India*, p. 831 (Modern World series).

The hands of the Nationalist are supposed to be strengthened by the machinery of the reforms. "Its purpose," says Lord Meston,

> is to habituate the old official executive, even in discharging its own responsibilities, to rely more and more upon the support of its Legislature and less and less upon the support of the British Parliament.[1]

Since the capture of many seats in the Legislature by the Congress Party the Councils have ceased to be docile to the Services, and the Services have fought hard against the encroachment of Ministers and the Councils.

[1] *The Dominions and Dependencies of the Empire*, p. 211.

PART II

TWO INDIAS

CONFLICT BETWEEN PRINCES AND PEOPLE—THE CROWN AS THE CONNECTING LINK

CHAPTER XI

NATIVE AUTOCRACY

THERE are over six hundred States [1] in India, varying in size and population from Hyderabad, which covers 82,698 square miles, with a population of 12,471,770 and a revenue of £4,600,000, to Maler Kotla, with an area of 168 square miles and a population of 80,332 and an approximate revenue of £100,000, and to Suket, which has an area of 420 square miles and a population of only 54,328 and an approximate revenue of £15,000.

All the States put together cover an area of 598,138 square miles, which is about two-fifths of the total area of the whole of India excluding Burma, which is 1,571,625 square miles. The States have a population of 68,652,974, nearly a quarter of the population of the whole country, which is 305,730,288.

The powers of the chiefs of one State differ from those of another, but the form of government may be described generally as personal and autocratic.

The *sunnuds*, or treaties, between the British Government and the States also differ, but in actual practice the differences have been of degree and not of kind. Hyderabad, which hugged the age-old superstition that it was an independent State in matters of internal administration, received a snub from Lord Reading, the Viceroy of India, which once for all disposed of the delusion of the rulers of

[1] The India Office List (1928) speaks of over six hundred States, whereas General Sir O'Moore Creagh, in his *Indian Studies* (p. 217), speaks of "some seven hundred feudatory States." J. D. Rees gives the actual figure in his *Real India* (p. 130) as 675, of which 175 are directly under the Government of India and 500 under the Provincial Government. The most reliable figure, however, must be that of the States Inquiry Committee, who group the States under three classes, numbering altogether 562.

the States as to their own and unlimited rights and privileges in internal matters.[1]

Lord Reading's warning caused considerable trepidation in India. It evoked the sympathy of the thoughtful people in British India. It was hailed with satisfaction by the subjects of the Hyderabad State, who were dissatisfied with the personal rule of the Nizam.

The Nizam had claimed that, save and except in matters relating to foreign Powers and policies, the Nizams of Hyderabad have been independent in the internal affairs of the State, just as much as the British Government. Lord Reading felt it was incumbent on him as his Imperial Majesty's representative to remove the gross misconception of the biggest of Indian Chiefs—a misconception under which the minor Princes have also been labouring. Lord Reading plainly warned the Nizam that the sovereignty of the British Crown was supreme in India, and therefore no ruler of an Indian State could justifiably claim to negotiate with the British Government on an equal footing. The Viceroy further indicated that the right of the British Government to intervene in the internal affairs of Indian States was another instance of the consequences necessarily involved in the supremacy of the British Crown.

The Princes did not like this unambiguous enunciation on the part of the ex-Lord Chief Justice of England of the legal power and moral right of Britain to interfere even in internal matters of administration within the States. Their own notions of their importance and independence have been embodied in a publication[2] in which they contrast the old policy of Britain with the new policy enunciated by

[1] Letter from the Viceroy and Governor-General of India to his Exalted Highness the Nizam of Hyderabad, dated Delhi, March 27, 1926. This letter is reprinted as an appendix to the *States Inquiry Committee Report*, 1928–29.

[2] *The British Crown and Indian States.* An Outline Sketch drawn up on behalf of the Standing Committee of the Chamber of Princes, by the Directorate of the Chamber's Special Organization (P. S. King and Son, Ltd., 1929).

Lord Reading. They quote from a letter of Lord Dalhousie in reply to a suggestion of General Fraser, British Resident in Hyderabad, that the Government of India should intervene to set affairs right in the Nizam's dominions.[1] Lord Dalhousie declined to interfere in the domestic affairs of the Nizam, though his dominions were groaning under the vices of gross misgovernment. Lord Dalhousie held that as long as the alleged evils of his Highness's Government were confined within its own limits and affected only his subjects "the Government of India must observe religiously the obligations of its own good faith."

Armed with these and other authorities, the Princes thought that they had a good case, and demanded an inquiry into their powers and status. They pressed their demand with success upon the British Government at a time when they were appointing the Parliamentary Commission to inquire into the conditions in British India in regard to the working of the constitutional reforms leading to Dominion status. The Princes claimed that if British India were to be given Dominion status there were important matters, besides their own status and prerogatives, such as their financial and economic relations with British India, which required exploration.

The Right Hon. the Earl of Birkenhead, in his capacity as Secretary of State for India, appointed on December 16, 1927, the Indian States Inquiry Committee under the Chairmanship of Sir Harcourt Butler, whom Lord Chelmsford in one of his Viceregal utterances had pleasantly described as "our political Don Juan."

The States Inquiry Committee submitted their report to the Right Hon. Viscount Peel, Lord Birkenhead's successor, who presented it to Parliament in March 1929.

As the Conservatives were defeated at the last General Election the task of taking whatever action his Majesty's Government might deem fit on the report and its findings

[1] *The British Crown and Indian States*, pp. 52, 53, 54.

fell on the Right Hon. Wedgwood Benn, Secretary of State for India. It must indeed be a rather curious experience for a Socialist Government to consider what attitude they should adopt toward the Princes and Chiefs of India—curious because Socialism is the antipodes of the institution of Princes, who are despotic monarchs in their own kingdoms, though vassals of a constitutional monarch.

The Indian States Inquiry Committee met with a cordial reception alike from the people and the Princes. This was a happy if dramatic contrast to the scenes which faced the Simon Commission in British India.

The subjects of the States wanted to place their grievances before the States Inquiry Committee. A States Deputation came to England with a view to approaching the Committee. But the Committee would not, because they could not, receive them. Contrast this with the fate of the Simon Commission issuing invitations to the Indian people, a ferocious and powerful section of which would not recognize or approach it, notwithstanding its sweet ways. The subjects of Indian States did not boycott the Butler Committee as the people of British India did the Simon Commission. It was the other way about. They felt that the Butler Committee had boycotted the State subjects.

This can only be explained as due to the extreme anxiety on the part of the Government not to encourage—or rather not to be suspected of encouraging—the subjects of the States to aspire to democracy, the one thing that the Princes fear.

The British Government's policy in regard to the States appears to be to Europeanize them by introducing in them more British men and methods. A suggestion has been made by the Butler Committee that a new States Service should be inaugurated corresponding, presumably, to the Indian Civil Service. Instead of instituting this new Service, it would save all pother if the Indian Civil Service were increasingly employed in the Indian States. Perhaps that does not fit in with the scheme of developing the States into an independent group—independent of a liberated British India, but very much dependent on his Majesty's Government in Great Britain.

Supposing some democratic Maharaja of the future wants to introduce responsible government in his State and reduce himself to the position of a constitutional monarch, will the Paramount Power agree to it or force him to abdicate, or intern him under the Bengal Regulation III of 1818 without a trial as too dangerously democratic and politically minded?

So far the British Government have shown no enthusiasm in inducing the Maharajas to make experiments in democracy, as Mr Montagu did in British India. So far they have not discouraged the Maharajas from putting down agitation in their own territory, even if it happens to be legitimate. The British policy in the past has been generally one of tolerance for the strength with which the Maharajas put down all inconvenient agitation and keep out all troublesome agitators. The Residents of these States were apt to show some sneaking admiration for the pursuit of 'repression' in the States. How long the Maharajas will keep out their subjects from their undoubted right, not only to participate in the administration, but to make it responsible to themselves, is more than one can predict. The difficulty of the State subject is greater than that of the British subject. The latter had to deal with a class of administrators who, whatever their anxiety—which is natural and human—not to part with power, had after all instinct in them the spirit of democracy to which they were born and under which they were bred. Again, the ultimate appeal of the British Indian subject was to the British democracy and its traditions. The State subject, on the other hand, has to deal with the Maharaja, whose traditions and instincts are opposed to democracy in any form. "Benevolent autocracy" is the *ne plus ultra* of perfection to which any State subject can aspire. The best Maharajas generally would like to play the *rôle* of benevolent despots, but where the Maharaja is good but weak, and the Dewan (Prime Minister) unscrupulous and strong, there is neither honesty nor justice nor fair play in the administration. British India, it is no exaggeration to say, is a thousand times better than the Native States, alike in the matter of justice and fair play.

Essentially foreign even now at the top, owing no responsibility to the people, the British Indian Government deals with the people, both individually and collectively, more justly than the States Government. The reason for this is that the British Government in India is not a wholly unresponsible body, but is responsible to Britain. Even when the British democracy was not so representative as to-day, even when the electorate was imperfect and undeveloped, Parliament watched with dismay and scrutinized with ruthless attention the doings of its rulers. A remarkable Empire-builder like Warren Hastings could not escape impeachment in the House of Commons. The Maharajas, however, have no such authority to fear. Their cruelties and excesses are ignored even when systematically exposed in the Nationalist Press in British India, which is not given an opportunity to establish its case by being proceeded against under the Princes Protection Act. The British Government are in the habit of showing tolerance to a Maharaja so long as he is not noted for his independence. So long as he is loyal to the Residents and behaves like a good boy they admonish him for some of his notorious acts, only privately and departmentally.[1]

Had it not been for the British there would have been such terrible riots and popular risings in the States that the unpopular Maharajas would have disappeared or been

[1] "Up with a good Rajah, down with a bad; most up with a very bad who brings in a British administrator."—*In India*, by G. W. Steevens, p. 249.

deprived of their autocratic powers. But the British Government cannot avoid, if need arises, helping these Maharajas, because they have deprived them of their militias, which they could have used against their rebellious subjects. The safety of the Maharajas therefore lies in the strength of the British Army, the fear of which prevents their subjects from entertaining the merest thought of rebellion.

Fierce is the conflict which has arisen in the States between the Princes and the people. The former cling ferociously to their inheritance of despotic power, while the latter are struggling for their right to evolve and control a popular constitution. This difficult matter was not tackled by the States Inquiry Committee. Theirs was the simpler task of reconciling the differences between the Princes and the Paramount Power in regard to the actual status and mutual relations of each to the other.

It is necessary to mention here that the people of the Indian States who desired that their representatives should be given a hearing by the States Inquiry Committee were not given an opportunity to present the case on the technical ground that the Committee's terms of reference did not include the grievances of the people. It is easy to blame the Committee for not having heard the people's deputation. Their report has been criticized as one-sided, based on the version of one party. But the Committee could not, constituted as they were, go into the bigger and more complicated problem of the internal administration of the States with particular reference to the aspirations of the State subjects. The fault lay with the terms of reference of the Committee, and not with the Committee itself.

His Majesty's Government were obviously concerned to handle a delicate problem in as cautious a way as possible. By making the terms of reference comprehensive and providing the subjects of the States with facilities to present their grievances before the Committee, his Majesty's Government would have assumed powers which the States or, more correctly, their rulers have either repudiated or resisted. The Committee's purpose was first to investigate the extent of the authority of the Paramount Power, and, secondly, to inquire into the financial and economic relations between British India and the States. The investigation has resulted in their cryptic conclusion, "Paramountcy must remain paramount." [1] In other words, the British authority is ultimate and final and must prevail in the Indian States, as in British India. The Paramount Power, says the Committee,

> must fulfil its obligations, defining or adapting itself according to the shifting necessities of the time and the progressive development of the States. Nor need the States take alarm at this conclusion. Through paramountcy and paramountcy alone have grown up and flourished those strong benign relations on which at times the States rely. On paramountcy and paramountcy alone can the States rely for their preservation through the generations that are to come. Through paramountcy is pushed aside the danger of destruction.[2]

Wise and carefully chosen words these, but pregnant with meaning. While in the above passages lurks a gentle hint about changing times and progressive development, and the duty of the States to move with the times—it is the function of the Paramount Power to see to it that they do so—there is also the imperceptible assurance that when the democratic movement becomes too strong for the States to resist they can rely on paramountcy to save them from "the danger of destruction."

The States Inquiry Committee is protecting the Princes against themselves. In their supreme folly the Princes claim independence from the British authority. They complain that the British yoke exercised through the

[1] *States Inquiry Committee Report*, par. 57, p. 31.
[2] *Ibid.*

Governor-General and his Agent has been lying heavy on their necks, that, according to the treaty rights and engagements, they are independent in internal matters, whereas actually the British interference has been harassing and improper.[1] By way of propaganda, 'boosting' the rights and claims of the Chiefs, the Directorate of the Chamber of Princes have also published a book[2] emphasizing the disabilities under which the rulers of the States labour owing to the endless surveillance of the British Government in internal matters.

The *States Inquiry Committee Report* is a courteous reply to the pretensions of the Princes who would have vanished—owing to the corruption of their judiciary[3] and the extravagant luxuries in which they irresponsibly waste public money—before a ruthless public awakening.

British interference in Indian States is necessary; but unfortunately at times it has been exercised with excessive restraint in the case of Princes who are reactionaries, and with excessive severity in the case of Princes who have democratic leanings. The old British bureaucrat liked the Oriental despot. Before the War the retired bureaucrat was never tired of singing the praises of the Princes. He has even attacked the policy of interference of the British officers in the internal affairs of the Princes, saying "Leave them alone; give them a free hand to do what they like in their States. They are their States, after all!" The admiration of the retired civilian for the Indian Chiefs and their uncontrolled rights has found expression in his writings. One of them deplored "the craze for reform

[1] "If a second Akhbar were born in India, we would not let him rule in his own way, and he would in that case rather not rule at all. It is childish to blame the Rajah for being Oriental."—*In India*, p. 249.

[2] *The British Crown and Indian States.*

[3] "A small party of Hindus called at the Mission bungalow to make a request on behalf of a friend who lived in one of the Native States. They affirmed that it was an impossibility to get justice in a law-court in one of these States except through the intervention of the British Resident."—*India and Indians*, by Edward Elwin, p. 119.

after British patterns" of the European officers in the States.[1] He has even accused them of forming a "little European clique" in the capital of the Princes, who could not resist "the temptation to introduce into native States those principles of administration which they have always practised" in British India.

This reactionary view no longer finds favour with the British officers of to-day. They are developing a new angle of vision, much to the distress of the pampered rulers of the States. Either the States must progress on modern and democratic lines with British India, or its rulers must agree to the constant interference and control of the Paramount Power in internal affairs.

The age of despotism has passed away in British India. If by a fiat of the Socialist Government in Britain all the Indian States were abolished none would be more happy than the subjects of the States themselves.[2]

The majority of Princes, instead of chafing at the intervention of the British Government, must feel grateful that their States have not been annexed to British India on the ground of maladministration. With the exception of some of the South Indian States, where English education has progressed as rapidly as in British India, owing to a succession of enlightened Princes who saw the wisdom of opening colleges affiliated to the British universities in their respective provinces, the administration of the Indian States is appallingly crude and indisputably corrupt.

One-man rule is bad enough even when the man is able, but when it degenerates into the rule of a man who is addicted to the worst vices of Oriental despotism—women, wine, and idle amusements at the cost of the people—it becomes a nightmare. Were a referendum taken to-day among the subjects they would cheerfully vote for the

[1] *Real India*, p. 135.

[2] "Many of their people would like to be annexed to British India."—*In India*, p. 249.

annexation of the States to British India. The States exist to-day because of the mercy of the British.

Had there been in British India one-thousandth of that corruption and dishonesty and oppression and uncontrolled autocracy you find in the Indian States, long ago the British *Raj* would have perished. But the tragedy is that the British *Raj* tolerates the Princes, who are notorious for their maladministration, as if to enable the Indian people by way of contrast to choose between two evils.[1] Between a tolerated and tolerable foreign rule and an intolerant and impossible native autocracy the choice is easy. No wonder British rule in India is more popular than that of the Maharajas! Tell Indians that England would to-morrow parcel out India into so many little States under Maharajas, and thus make the whole of India hitherto directly under the British as self-governing as the States, and see what happens! A whole country will rise in revolt against that shocking suggestion. Take away the protecting arm of Britain from these medieval Maharajas and their subjects, who have been groaning under their unspeakable meanness and tyranny, will overthrow them in one single week.

British India is not a heaven, though the European officials there sometimes act like little divinities and infallibles. They are, in the Right Hon. J. Ramsay MacDonald's satirical words, "imperious and imperial."[2] But they have begun to feel that the power which made them near to gods must vanish. It is decreasing fast. If British India is not a heaven the Indian States are a veritable hell.[3] There is only one way to improve them.

[1] "We might annex them—there is never any lack of pretext—and we might leave them entirely alone to serve as awful examples and make our subjects (in British India) contented by the contrast."—*In India*, pp. 249, 250.

[2] *The Awakening of India*, by J. Ramsay MacDonald.

[3] Lord Curzon wrote: "One Prince . . . was a confirmed drunkard, shot his servant dead in a fit of ungovernable temper; another was privy to the poisoning of his uncle; a third . . . for nearly twenty years had been

And that is to make the rulers constitutional kings—subject to the suzerainty of the British Crown in external affairs, and to the will of the people in internal administration. That is the only answer that can be given to the Princes' demand for independence from British interference. That answer has not been given by the Indian States Inquiry Committee, which was only charged with the professorial *rôle* of interpreting in the light of existing documents the powers of paramountcy. Will that aspect be examined by the Reforms Inquiry Commission presided over by Sir John Simon, now that the scope of its inquiry has been extended? A joint or separate consultation of the political leaders and the Princes in the neighbourhood of Whitehall may have some value if the question can be approached boldly. But the real responsibility of introducing responsible government in the Indian States rests with the Paramount Power. The States Inquiry Committee have shirked it. But it cannot be shirked for long. The Maharajas, who are generally perverse and ill-educated, are not the sort of people who will like to follow the example of the Samurai of Japan, who voluntarily relinquished their power.[1] They have to be forced to move with the times.

Perhaps realizing that this step is not possible, the States Inquiry Committee, after establishing with weighty proofs the sovereignty of the suzerain power, suggests that a new set of British political officers, recruited from the universities and given special training, should go forth to the

guilty of gross maladministration, of shocking barbarity in the treatment of his subjects."—*Leaves from a Viceroy's Notebook, and other Papers*, by the Marquess Curzon of Kedleston, p. 42.

[1] "As a fine old Sikh, the Raja of Nabha, said to me: 'We educate our sons, teach them English and Western ideas, and then marry them to girls who have had no education. The result will be a breed of mules.'"—*The India we Served*, by Sir Walter Lawrence, p. 111.

"The education of chiefs, moreover, has not been conspicuously successful, because youths have been brought up to be English rather than Indian and to hanker after visits to England rather than residence among their own people."—*Real India*, p. 137.

Native States. It is also suggested that these young officers might at some early period in their career be attached to the British Embassies or Ministries.[1] The present political officers, the Report concedes, have been good, but the desire is to secure a better class with a better knowledge of the customs of the people and all those graceful courtesies of manner and conduct to which Indians attach supreme importance. This recommendation does not go to the root of the matter. What is wanted is opportunity for the people of the States to control the administration. Public control is the only cure against nepotism and despotism—the two things which are blasting the life and aspirations of the State subjects. And the British *Raj* will be rendering a great service if it does not side with the Princes as against the people in regard to the latter's aspirations to have the same reforms which their neighbours enjoy under the British. If the British *Raj* goes a step farther in the right direction, and compels the Princes to transfer power to their subjects, at least to the same extent as in British India, it would be laying the foundations of democracy in the most backward and misgoverned parts of the British Empire.

[1] *States Inquiry Committee Report*, par. 75.

CHAPTER XII

THE CLAMOUR OF THE PRINCES

An important official committee appointed by the British Government discovered the existence of "two Indias"![1] The Government themselves had recognized inwardly—though they wanted probably a committee to explore the fact and give vent to its opinion with the weight of strenuous investigation—that the time had arrived to tell the politicians of the advanced school in British India, who were clamouring for sovereign independence for India and a policy of 'clean cut,' of complete separation from England, that India was only a geographical expression; that the India which was ruled by the British directly, the Government of which territory was constitutionally responsible to the British electorate in Great Britain, was not the same as the India which was ruled by the Indian Chiefs, whose relations with the Paramount Power were embodied in treaties; that "British India," as the former was called, was promised in the fullness of time full responsible government. This was different from endowing the whole of India with Dominion status, because India was not a Dominion—in fact, India never existed—there were two Indias—and the only India which could be treated as a Dominion was British India, which could not be related to the rest of the country any more than Ulster could be to the Irish Free State.

Whatever the possibilities or impossibilities of the new Independence movement which has been set on foot in India by two schools of thought—the violent or frankly revolutionary and the non-violent Congress—it has made the ruling Chiefs—such of those who are members of the Princes'

[1] *States Inquiry Committee Report* (1928–29), par. 106.

Chamber—meet in solemn conclave and issue a definite warning that whereas they were in full sympathy with the aspirations and activities which are legitimate and loyal of the Indian politicians they had no sympathy whatever with the disloyal movement of independence, and were bound to resist it, should necessity arise, as loyal vassals of his Majesty the King-Emperor.[1]

The warning of the ruling chiefs seemed to have quick effect on the Allahabad [2] politicians of the Congress school, who delighted to masquerade as revolutionaries, and upon whom the real revolutionaries of Bengal looked with unfeigned contempt. Hurriedly these extreme masqueraders, almost in panic, joined hands with the avowedly moderate parties in the country—whom their jackals in the Press had always ridiculed for singing *Rule Britannia* with the faith of a true Imperialist—and produced what they were pleased to describe as "the All-Parties Report," by which they meant all those parties who, having abstained from co-operating with the British Parliamentary Commission purely on the ground that Indians were excluded from it, wanted at the same time to place their views before the British democracy.

This report was, curiously enough, praised generously by Sir John Simon, the Chairman of the British Commission, in public.[3] It was repudiated by the boycotting Sikhs and by a large section of the boycotting Muslims on the ground that it failed to do justice to the minorities; by the Princes on the ground that it did not understand their position; and by the revolutionaries on the ground that the *pundit* who led the Swaraj Party had sold the pass by recognizing the overlordship of Great Britain.

The report likewise evaded the question of Home Defence, without which Home Rule must be a far-off, adorable dream.

[1] *Proceedings* of the Chamber of Princes early in 1929.
[2] Headquarters of Nehru, the Swaraj Party leader.
[3] *The Dilemma in India*, by Sir Reginald Craddock, p. 229.

The failure of the Indian politicians to produce an agreed report is no argument or justification for leaving the Indian problem unsettled. How far the British Commission will go to solve the Indian problem remains to be seen. The States Inquiry has not contributed to the solution of the problem beyond indicating that there are " two Indias." It does not say that the two Indias will not unite, that " never the twain shall meet." It has mentioned a fact—an outstanding one. Perhaps it was not expected to peer far into the future and suggest the welding of the two Indias into one united whole at this stage. It is difficult to predict how far Sir John Simon and his colleagues will venture to handle this baffling question which they have not studied because it was not in the original scope of their inquiry.

Most likely, beyond a general observation on the existing state of things, they would with characteristic caution and prudence concentrate on the next stage in the growth of reforms in British India, especially in the provinces.

But the goal of Indian nationalism is one united India. If this can be secured under the shadow of the British flag it will redound to the credit of Indian and British statesmanship.

Ways and means will have to be found sooner or later to bring the Indian States and British India into a common federation. As it is, all the States themselves have not joined the Narendra Mandel, or Chamber of Princes. Pride and suspicion keep some of the prominent States, such as Mysore and Hyderabad, out of the Chamber of Princes. Their presence in the Chamber cannot be enforced any more than revolutionary organizations could be induced to recognize the British-made legislatures of the land, admission to which involves the affirmation of the oath of allegiance to the King, his heirs and successors. Yet the Princes who are loyal, like Mysore and Hyderabad, should have had no difficulty in attending the Chamber and participating in its deliberations. That they have held aloof from it is explained by the fact that they are unwilling to come down to the level of the minor Princes. This boycotting aloofness may be likened to a major province unwilling to recognize association with a minor province and therefore abstaining from sending its representatives to India's Parliament! Such a thing will certainly be absurd. It has only to be mentioned to be ridiculed. It has not arisen in British India, and is not likely to arise. Similarly the major States who have 'boycotted' the Chamber of Princes, not with the loud execration of political extremists, but with the quiet dignity of Oriental potentates, will have soon to fall into line, so that there can be the evolution of one Indian India, as it were, governed by the same ideas and ideals and the same system of government, more in keeping with this age, in which popular opinions must prevail, than with an age when absolutism swayed. Thus when the United States of India have been evolved with a satisfactory system of government, in which the inhabitants thereof will have the controlling voice, they can hope to take an equal place with the more advanced British India in the supreme Legislature of a United Indian Empire.

At present, as the States are divided among themselves, and British India from the States, this must remain a vision and a dream. This supreme Imperial Legislature cannot come into being so long as the Chamber of Princes is a farce, as now, which major Princes boycott, and in which the members themselves have been more concerned with the forming of a kind of Trade Union with a view to protecting the so-called sovereign rights of Princes—long extinct in practice, though not in theory—and to preventing the encroachments of the Paramount Power and its ubiquitous representative in the person of the Resident or the Agent to the Governor-General. When the Princes have learned to unite and lay down common laws to the satisfaction of their people, when in their Chamber they resolve to part with power, when they, in short, follow the good example of their sovereign the King-Emperor, who is a constitutional monarch, when they cease to clamour against interference of the Paramount Power by making that interference impossible by themselves becoming constitutional, it can be said that Indian India may be trusted to co-operate with British India as an equal partner in the Indian Imperial Federation, and prove a rare instrument of human good. As it is, the Chiefs are despots—either petty or mighty according to the size of their territory. Lest they should abuse their arbitrary powers they have been kept under the vigilant eye of the Paramount Power. The Paramount Power itself will desire to continue its vigilance, not because authority is always pleasing and the exercise thereof is a constant reminder of the supremacy of British rule, but in the interests of the Princes and their subjects alike. The Princes have been complaining that treaty rights have been ignored and their authority impaired even in internal administration by the intervention of the Resident. They secured costly legal advice from one of the most eminent lawyers in England, who pronounced his opinion that the treaty rights were sacred and the relations of the Princes should be directly with the Crown.[1] The Paramount Power however, which represents the Crown does not deny the sacredness of the *sunnuds* (treaties), but only maintains that paramountcy must be paramount.[2]

In the declaration of the British supremacy over the Princes the Paramount Power carries with it the sympathy of the numerous subjects of the Princes who have been living under their grinding—at best benevolent—despotism, with no voice or choice in the administration.

The Princes do not recognize that times have changed all over the world and that the old order must change also in the States; that it is useless to look up to treaties which were made under different conditions and on the interpretation of which they and the Paramount Power always differed.

If the Princes actually feel the interference of the Para-

[1] *The British Crown and Indian States.*

[2] "The rulers of these little States exercise more moral control over the people than all our magistrates, except in so far as *it is our Government which is paramount to their Rulers.*"—*The Prince of Wales' Tour in India, Greece, Egypt, Spain, and Portugal* (1877), by W. H. Russell, p. 425 (second edition).

mount Power· they must recognize that the only way to reduce it, and eventually altogether get rid of it, is for them courageously to agree to divest themselves of their power even as the Indian Civil Service. At present, when they desire that the British Authority should relax its control over them, they only demand the power to do as they like in the States.[1]

To please the democratic desires of their subjects, Legislatures have been set up in some of the States, but they are only debating societies. "I have got a Council," said the Maharaja of Bikaner to Mr Lloyd George, "but I nominate my Councillors."[2] The British Government do not interfere here and say, "No, you must give real power to your subjects." All that Britain does is to see to it that the Prince who has the power of a giant over his voiceless subjects does not use it as a giant. And Britain feels that it cannot relinquish its responsibility to the citizens of the Indian States, who are, after all, subjects of the King-Emperor, though not direct.

The King's Government is thus supreme in British India as well as in the Indian States. Only the form and method of government differ. In British India the Government is carried on by a different body, either responsible to the British Parliament, as in the past, or to the Indian people, as contemplated in the future. In the Indian States the Nawab, the Nizam, or the Maharaja carries on the Government, and is permitted to carry it on so long as he does not incur the displeasure of the Crown as represented by the Crown's agent, the Viceroy, and the Viceroy's agent, the Resident.[3]

[1] Lord Mayo, in his Viceregal address to the Great Darbar in Rajputana, enunciated British policy toward the States thus: "Be just and merciful to your people. We do not ask whether you come to us with full hands, but whether you come with clean hands."—*The British Crown and Indian States*, p. 63.

[2] Mr Lloyd George happened to convey this interesting information to the present writer at a luncheon in the House of Commons.

[3] "Many of the States are governed almost independently by their own rulers, but they are all subject in a greater or less degree to supervision and guidance at the hands of the British Government."—*The India Office List*, 1928, p. 579.

CHAPTER XIII

AN INTRIGUING FUTURE

JUDGING first from the physical features of India, two great divisions are noticeable, the first comprising the true Indian peninsula, and the second the mountain-belt which includes the Himalayan highlands and hills of Kashmir, Baluchistan, and Burma.

Judging, secondly, from the religious point of view, two Indias emerge, that of the Hindu and that of the Muslim, which communities have unfortunately nothing in common with each other, such as social relations or intermarriage. Their segregation is enforced by the isolating barrier of religion. According to the Census report,[1] the adherents of the Hindu religion number so many as 216,734,586, whereas the Mussulmans number 68,735,233 out of a population of 318,942,480.

Judging from the ethnographic point of view, there are in India two pronounced types, the Indo-Aryan and the Turko-Iranian, or Semitic, besides the pure Indian and the pure Iranian. The pure Indians, or aborigines, are a primitive people, numbering 9,774,611, whom the Aryan tyranny of caste had condemned as untouchable and put beyond the pale of society, whereas the pure Iranians, who are an ornament and an asset to the country, found a welcome refuge in India when they fled from the tyranny of the Muslim tyrants of Persia. The Parsees are pure Iranians, profess Zoroastrianism, and number 101,778. They generally marry only among themselves, and are an exclusive and wealthy community. The only marriage in high circles of a Parsee girl with a Muslim barrister created a

[1] The Census of 1921 being the latest.

storm in the Parsee community. There have been no recognized intermarriages of the Aryan settlers in India with the aborigines, though there has been considerable intermixture between the Aryans and the higher native caste, forming an Aryo-Dravidian, or Hindustani, type. There is also a Mongolo-Dravidian type, from which the Muslims of Eastern Bengal and the Hindus of Orissa and Lower Bengal are drawn.

The Indo-Aryans consist, besides Hindus, of 11,571,268 Buddhists, 3,238,803 Sikhs, and 1,178,596 Jains. The Turko-Iranians, besides Muslims, include a small population of 21,778 Jews. There are 4,754,064 followers of another Semitic religion, Christianity, but for the most part this class is drawn from the aborigines and the depressed classes of India.

From an educational point of view there are two Indias, the literate and the illiterate. But the size of illiterate India is gradually decreasing, and when it disappears it can be said that India has become one. In 1911 only 59 per 1000 could read and write. In 1921, 82 per 1000 were literate. Of these, again, in 1911 only one male in 9·5 and one female in 96 could read and write. For every 10,000 there were 160 males and 18 females who could be classed as literate in 1921, as compared with 95 males and 10 females per 10,000 in 1911.

The administrative division of two Indias is the India directly governed by the British and the States, which are governed by the Indian Chiefs. The British provinces have a population of 247,003,293 and the Indian States 71,939,187.

The British territories comprise roughly three-fifths of the area of India and over three-fourths of its population.

While two Indias are thus visible there is yet the hope of their being and becoming one under the guidance of the British Empire, if India's future is to be peacefully evolved. At present the Indian Chiefs govern the States with the assistance of the British Government, who supervise the administration of the States through their political officers, who are responsible to the Political Department directly under the Governor-General himself. Owing to the oft-expressed desire of the Princes to be directly associated with the Crown and liberated from the clutches of British India fast coming into its own, it is in contemplation to make the Political Department an exclusively Viceregal portfolio, the Viceroy as the representative of the Crown being apart, in theory, from the Governor-General, who is the head of the administration and whose functions might be ultimately taken up by the Prime Minister of a self-governing India.[1]

The Indian rulers of the States have been given ample freedom by the British Government—so long as they are loyal—to carry on the administration of the country according to their whim and fancy. They possess vast revenues, and are in the habit of treating them as their own private income and the State itself as their own private property. They exercise the power of life and death over their subjects. But they have no power, as in olden times, to make war upon each other, because their suzerain in India, which is the British Government, does not allow them to indulge in that luxury. Nor have they the power to enter into alliances with foreign countries. It was the dream of the Nizam of Hyderabad to enter into an alliance with the Amir of Afghanistan before Amanullah's fall, as his Exalted Highness had not exhausted his superstitious faith in his own independence, which he fancied was equal to that of the King of the Afghan tribes. Promptly, however, the Nizam was told, as we have seen, by the Governor-General that it was dangerous for a subordinate to dream dreams!

No longer can the hereditary Indian Chiefs say with the last of the Kaisers, as in the days before the British came to India, when they ruled their own territories and waged war against each other as the European countries:

[1] Which means British India.

AN INTRIGUING FUTURE

> I am resolved to keep the peace with every one so far as in *Me* lies, but woe to him who shall dare to offend *Me.*[1]

This was the first Coronation Declaration of Kaiser Wilhelm II, but in India the coronation itself is impossible until the legitimacy of the Princes is recognized by the British Government. What is more, the coronation itself must be formally approved, even of a legitimate heir to the *Gadi*, by the Paramount Power.

The British Government rebukes bad Princes, however exalted they may be. It dethrones independent ones, because a spirit of independence so long as it is directed against the people of the States matters not, but when it is manifested against the authority of the suzerain or its representative, the political agent, woe to that Indian Prince!

Where then do the two Indias come? There is only one India in reality, the India of the British Crown.[2]

In one sense the real British India is that of the States, where powerful British officers can exercise more authority by reducing the Princes to the *rôle* of honorary magistrates, if they care, though they are willing to patronize these pampered dolls. Similar power cannot be exercised unquestioned by British officials and District Officers in India, for their action is immediately the subject of a volley of questions in the Legislatures.

Why should the Indian States not pass under the control of the Indian Government of the future when self-government is granted? Because the Indian rulers like their present position, which cannot last for a single day when politicians dominate Simla-Delhi, for, true to their faith, they would have to consult the people of the States as to the form of government there. The subjects of the States, loyal and conservative by nature, will not as a whole vote for the

[1] *Kaiser Wilhelm II, from Birth to Exile*, by Emil Ludwig.
[2] *States Inquiry Committee Report*, par. 18.

abolition of monarchy, but would certainly insist on the Maharajas becoming constitutional.

The Maharajas to-day have ample freedom to govern wrong and ride roughshod over their people.[1] They can hire a score of rooms in the most expensive hotels in England, and spend a million pounds upon any woman whom they fancy or who succeeds in fooling them. Such a thing will not be tolerated by any Legislature in the land. While willing to parade their loyalty to the King of England, their Emperor, the Maharajas are unwilling to follow his good example and become constitutional rulers. And so long as constitutional rule is not introduced in the States there will be two Indias, the India of the tyrannical Maharajas who thrive on British help and can resist the aspirations of the people, and the India of the politicians who want to copy the ways of the advanced West and themselves govern the country with the sanction of the people.

The two Indias must and will continue, so long as there is democracy in the one and despotism in the other. If, to-day, they are answerable to a common Government it is on the basis of autocracy. The British Government in India is autocratic, from the Indian standpoint, because it is not responsible to the people of India. Its responsibility is to the British Parliament, and through them to the British electorate. And so long as the responsibility is not transferred from the British to the Indian electorate it can govern the States and the people alike. But as a definite move is being made in the direction of the transference of responsibility, a corresponding move is also made on the chessboard of diplomacy. If India is to be self-governing it will only be that part of India which is directly governed by

[1] "The more important of these Princes exercise the power of life and death over their subjects."—*The Indian Empire*, by Sir W. W. Hunter, p. 76.

"Now the protected autocrat in a Native State has not as yet turned out such a success that the English nation can feel proud of having brought him out upon the political stage."—*Asiatic Studies*, by Sir Alfred C. Lyall, p. 225 (second edition).

the British. Not the other part, which is ruled by the Maharajas, who wish to be ruled from Whitehall more than from Simla-Delhi.

Up till now the Dewans and other State administrators have been drawn from the educated classes in India who did not find adequate scope for their energy and competence in British India. Now that opportunities for the educated Indians are coming in a flood with the reforms the product of the English universities are to be given a greater scope in the States.[1]

There has been so far only one India. Henceforward there must be two Indias. Though chafing under the surveillance of political agents, the Princes are unwilling to come under the direct control of the Government of a free India of the future.[2] This will suit the British Government. The States will have an army in the future—manned by the British—when India has her own army. The States will have their own British Services when India has her Indian Services. The States, in fact, will be responsible to the Crown—that is to say, the Viceroy and his Political Department, for the Viceroy cannot govern without a department to help him. And this department for all time to come will be apart from the other departments of the Government of India, and above them so far as international obligations and relations are concerned, international because India consists of two nations, those who live in the States and those in British India. It is no longer a Hindu and a Muslim India. This racial division—not unknown to other self-governing lands where there are more races than one—is bound to disappear with the advance of time and the operations of democracy, as it tended to disappear in England itself, where the Protestants reconciled themselves to the Catholics. The race cleavage was finally obliterated with the removal of the Jewish disabilities by an Act of Parliament. But not so easily can the

[1] *States Inquiry Committee Report*, par. 75. [2] *Ibid.*, par. 58.

political division and the hold of vested interests disappear. Long, if not perpetual, will the cleavage be between British India, which will under self-government become Indian India, and the Indian States of to-morrow, which will be the real British India of yesterday. But there is nothing perpetual in life—nothing permanent in history. Human ingenuity can provide only so far as it sees. Eastern philosophers do not think of the morrow. Wise Westerners provide against a rainy day. The means which British and bureaucratic ingenuity has devised is to separate the functions of the Viceroy and Governor-General [1] when the day comes, transferring to the former the power which the latter holds to-day over the States, when the rest of his present power will be transferred to the Prime Minister of India. As the relations between British India and the States are intricate, and have every chance of straining, eternal vigilance over them is necessary, and the Viceroy will serve that purpose, acting for the Crown, which, unlike the coronets in Indian States, means Parliament,[2] as England is "a crowned Republic." [3]

The future is really intriguing. The best way to make things smooth is to convert the autocrats of the States into constitutional chiefs. But Britain is not interested in forcing unwilling Princes, who already complain of excessive interference. Britain's only purpose is to follow the line of least resistance. The only remedy is for a democratic Prince of some future date to arise and voluntarily transfer his power, reducing himself to the position of a constitutional ruler, and his own State to that of a crowned republic under the British Crown. Until that happy day comes—as come it must—the best thing for the people in British India is to mind their own business. A self-governing British India—and the long road to self-government, which has yet to be travelled, is not

[1] *States Inquiry Committee Report*, par. 67. [2] *Ibid.* par. 18.
[3] H. G. Wells, in his *Outline of History*.

strewn with roses—will have much work to do within its own domain.

The best stimulus to the growth of self-government within the States themselves is successful self-government all round in its own neighbourhood. The growth of reforms and of the power of the Legislatures in British India has witnessed a new awakening in the States' subjects. Self-government cannot be imposed—whether in British India or the Indian States—from outside. It must come from within. And when it so comes India will be moulded into one united whole, as never before in its history, under one Federal Government, self-governing on the whole, and each State and province in its own compass self-governed.[1]

[1] "Following the American constitution rather than the British . . . we must work genuinely to create south of the Himalayas *the United States of Hindustan.*"—*The Observer*, Sunday, February 2, 1930.

CHAPTER XIV

INDIA'S ULSTERS

THERE are "two Indias," even as there are two Irelands. This is a fact which both the British and the Indian peoples cannot obliterate from their minds while dealing with the Indian problem.

Parliament's and the King's pledge of responsible government, *Swaraj*, or Dominion Home Rule, was given to his Majesty's Indian subjects not as distinct from the subjects of his Majesty's subordinates, or vassals, known as Indian Chiefs. This is made clear by the Viceroy's Proclamation of November 1929.

A United India under one Government has not been known to India's past. Anything resembling a United India under the British sovereignty we may vainly search for in the pages of history. India to-day is far from united. The Indian Chiefs, while professing sympathy [1] with the aspirations of their countrymen in British India, have done nothing to promote the same aspirations in their own subjects. Nor have they missed an opportunity to warn their countrymen in British India against following whatever course they might choose in politics or enunciating whatever ideals they might cherish as the goal of their political ambition.

In 1929, when the Congress began to dream of independence in despair, the Princes plainly told the people in British India that the dream was uncanny. It was

[1] The Standing Committee of the Chamber of Princes unanimously adopted a resolution at Bombay in March 1928, reaffirming "on the one hand, the loyalty of the Indian States to the Crown and their attachment to the Empire, and, on the other hand, their sympathy with the aspirations of British India, which they regard as legitimate."

almost a nightmare. It conflicted with their own loyalty to the Throne. They proclaimed that they would resist independence should occasion arise even at the risk of bloodshed.

The history of India under British rule shows that in the great Indian Mutiny of 1857, the day of commencement of which was observed last year by the advanced school of Indian politicians as "the Indian War of Independence Day," the Princes stood staunchly by Britain. Lord Canning was happy to confess that a few patches of Native Government proved "breakwaters to the storm which would otherwise have swept over us in one great wave." [1]

Gandhi made no secret of appealing to the patriotism of the Indian soldiers in 1921. Should 1857 repeat itself, should India make a bid for a revolution, the British Government naturally look to the Princes to prove "breakwaters." The Princes are quite willing to play their loyal part should necessity arise. An indication of this was given by the proceedings of the Chamber of Princes early in 1929, in which in unequivocal language they condemned the movement in British India for sovereign independence and severance of all connexion with England.

It is natural that the British Government, while relaxing their hold on British India, should draw the Indian States closer to themselves. All apprehensions of the Imperialists that Home Rule for British India would spell disaster to Great Britain and the Empire would be set at rest if only they realized that for several long years Home Rule in its completeness can mean no more than the status of the Irish Free State overshadowed by Ulster. India being

[1] *Last Counsels of an Unknown Counsellor*, by Major Evans Bell (John Dickinson; London, 1883).

Lord Roberts wrote on September 30, 1896: "The Mutiny was not an unmitigated evil, for to it we owe the consolidation of our power in India. . . . It was the Mutiny which brought Lord Canning into closer communication with the Princes of India and paved the way for Lord Lytton's brilliant conception of the Imperial Assemblage—a great political success which laid the foundation of that feeling of confidence which now, happily, exists between the ruling Chiefs and the Queen-Empress."—*Forty-one Years in India*, by Lord Roberts (Preface to the first edition).

an infinitely bigger country than Ireland, the Imperialists may be content to feel that India's Ulsters will be strong, vast, and many, scattered all over the country from the Himalayas to Cape Comorin, from Baluchistan to the Burmese frontier.

British India is only British in name; it is, in fact, aspiring to be more Indian than the States, the slogan of her politicians being Indianization of the Services and the Army. It is also in British India that the most anti-British speeches are delivered. They will continue to be so delivered until British India is accorded the same status as the Dominions enjoy. This is also incidentally the highest tribute to the English education which Britain imparted to India, fully conscious that a day would come when India would aspire to the same free life and full status as England herself.

So long as the Indian States do not keep abreast with the currents and movements in British India they will submit to the present system of autocracy. But its days are numbered. If the Princes are wise and do not rely too much on British protection they will agree to copy the British example in their own kingdoms and transfer their power to their subjects, just as Britain is divesting herself of her power, which the Indian people are beginning to exercise through their elected representatives in the Legislatures, both Central and Provincial.

The British Government themselves have given the Princes broad indications from time to time that they must bury the ancient ideas of autocracy and govern on modern lines. Britain will not be able to do much to accelerate the march of political development in the States. Her policy has been one of non-intervention as far as possible. But the clamour of their subjects for Parliamentary rule is making an impression even upon men who are respected by the Indian Government and who hold high offices under the Crown.

There are two conflicting ideas on the public mind in regard to the States. Those who do not believe in the good intentions of the British suspect that the British plan is to unite the States into an Ulster and thus divide India. Others who believe in Britain's good intentions feel that England aspires to protect the Princes so far as she may by ensuring their independence from British Indian interference in the States in internal politics when the former has attained Dominion status.[1] While giving the Princes that much security from the extravagant attentions which ambitious but inconvenient politicians might be inclined to show, Britain decidedly wants to keep them under control and treat them as subordinates, lest history should repeat itself and the Princes should either make war on each other or combine to wage war on British India, reducing the country to China's plight.[2]

The position of the Indian States, therefore, will be one of equality with British India, but subordination to Britain. A liberated British India will also have to be likewise subordinate to Britain in matters affecting British India and Indian States, such as boundaries, customs, railways, mints and currency, salt, posts, telegraphs, wireless and telephones, excise, etc., etc.

England will thus be the *Ma-Bap* (" the father and the mother ") of the two Indias until they see their way to unite into one.

Can they at all at any time unite? And if so, when? The answers to these questions naturally take the shape of prophecies. The ideal of every true Indian patriot is a United and Free India, an ideal which would have been easy to attain if the States had never come into existence,

1 " Princes should not be handed over without their agreement to a new government in India responsible to an Indian Legislature."—*States Inquiry Committee Report* (1928–29), par. 58 (His Majesty's Stationery Office).

2 " That Government, as suzerain in India, does not allow its feudatories to make war upon each other, or to have any relations with foreign States."—*The Indian Empire*, p. 76.

or had the country been parcelled out into States, big or small, under ruling chiefs responsible to the people.

All that, however, is out of the question at present. England will not be inclined to hand over British India to new Chiefs, nor will British India, which has been accustomed to a different kind of rule, agree to go back to medieval autocracy. India must therefore develop in two distinct directions, the States passing from benevolent despotisms to constitutional monarchies when British India passes from a bureaucratic to a wholly democratic form of government. When they have thus emerged they might think of coming under a common federation.

CHAPTER XV

A DILEMMA?

"The Princes and Chiefs of India," explains one of their sympathizers, "are in a serious quandary," [1] because they welcome democracy in British India, but contend that it is not suitable in their States. This, then, is a quandary of their own creation.

Democracy is less necessary in British India than in the Indian States, because the foreign bureaucrat is an Englishman, whereas the indigenous autocrat can degenerate, to borrow Sir Reginald Craddock's own words, into "a besotted despot." [2] The Indian Prince—unlike the Englishman with his democratic upbringing and spirit of freedom which carries with it adequate restraint—is first and last a despot.

A disgusted English writer speaks of Oriental despotism in language which would seem an exaggeration, but is wholly true of several of the Indian Princes and their out-of-date and tyrannical administration: "Indeed, Asiatic despotism, it must be said, has ever been and ever will be the worst throughout the world." [3]

Small wonder that the Princes do not contemplate with equanimity the prospect of their being made responsible to the self-governing India of the future. Only a "dreamer in an armchair," says the sympathizer of the Princes, "can believe that a peaceful settlement of the Indian States could be attained by making them as a class subordinate to a Parliament of Indian politicians." The Parliament of self-governing India will be as democratic as the British Parliament. The Princes are absolute rulers—autocrats of

[1] *The Dilemma in India*, by Sir Reginald Craddock, p. 96. [2] *Ibid.*
[3] *Pen and Pencil Sketches*, by W. H. Floris, p. 3 (Hutchinson).

the medieval type. Autocracy hates democracy. The Princes will not come under the sway or jurisdiction of British India in a hurry.

To avoid responsibility to the Indian Parliament cannot ensure immunity to the Princes from many kinds of responsibility. They must be responsible to their subjects within and suzerain without. In plain words they must be prepared to introduce the same democracy in their States which they applaud in British India, and abide, so far as internal administration is concerned, by the verdict of that democracy, accepting the same position in their States which constitutional practice has assigned to their liege lord, his Majesty the King-Emperor. In matters external they owe responsibility to the Crown, which will be represented in India, as we have seen, by the Viceroy,[1] the King's representative, assisted by the Political Department.

The most perplexing dilemma, one would have thought, is the Indian State. But the easiest way out is the introduction of responsible government in the States by reducing the Princes from despotic rulers to constitutional chiefs.[2]

In case the Maharajas and Nawabs and Nizams do not agree to introduce Parliaments and responsible Cabinets the only alternative is to make them responsible to the Government of India through the Residents, whose powers of intervention in State affairs must be increased.

The Viceroy—*i.e.*, his Political Department—through his Agent in the States must appoint the judges in the States. It is a notorious fact that there is no justice in the British

[1] *States Inquiry Committee Report.*

[2] Sir Reginald Craddock, in his recent book, *The Dilemma in India* (p. 89), says that "The Indian Princes and Chiefs can hardly be expected to transfer their allegiance from the British Crown to a collection of political notables drawn from various provinces of British India . . . any more than the barons who owed allegiance to the Plantagenet kings would have agreed in those days to bow their heads to a body of burgesses and attorneys." But Sir Reginald avoids the way out of the dilemma, which is not to transfer power from the Crown to an outside body, but to share their present power of internal administration with an elected Parliament, while in external matters continue to be under the direct suzerainty of the Crown until the evolution of the "Greater India" foreshadowed in the Viceregal Proclamation of October 1929.

sense of the term in the States. It is also a fact that the rulers are in the habit of interfering with the course of justice, especially in cases in which they or their favourites—which species abound in the States—are concerned. The appointment of European and I.C.S. judges must be preferred generally, and in every case the Chief Justice must be a Briton.

This suggestion is not an aspersion or reflection on the capacity or character of Indian judges.[1] But in the interests alike of the reputation of the Indian judges, as well as of justice itself, the difficult task must be allotted in the States in the present position of affairs—if democracy is not to be introduced in the States—to the English I.C.S. man. Behind the British judge will be the British Resident or Agent. Behind the Resident or Agent will be the Political Department of the Viceroy, his Majesty's representative in India. Therefore, the native rulers will abandon their old habit of influencing the judges.

It may be asked, are there not strong enough Indians who will put up a stubborn fight in case the ruler tries to influence the administration of justice? The answer is in the affirmative. Then it may be further asked, "Why should Britons be exclusively invited for the Chief Justiceship?" The answer is, the Maharaja will be afraid of approaching a British judge. He will not be afraid of approaching an Indian judge, so long as his powers are not transferred to his subjects through a representative Cabinet. Traditions can nowhere be easily altered or destroyed. They are stubborn in the East. And it is the tradition of the Maharajas to be the fountain of justice! The fountain must cease to be polluted. The presence of a strong Briton as the head of the judiciary is therefore an absolute necessity in the transitional stage.

Among other things, the Dewans, or Prime Ministers, of the States must also be Englishmen belonging to the

[1] In the British High Courts and subordinate courts Indian judges have proved themselves worthy of their position.

Indian Civil Service. It may be asked, "Have not Indians done great work and attained distinction in the States?" Yes, and their number is legion. Why then this change? When Indians did not have opportunities in British India, when at the top was the Englishman in every department, Indians of calibre found opportunities in the States. Now under the reforms era Indians have abundance of opportunities, they dominate every department except the Army and the police, in which, too, they have ambitions of domination which are certainly legitimate and cannot long be delayed. The Briton in the Civil Services who finds it difficult to get on with the Swarajist democracy can certainly be given a career in the congenial States.

When Indianization of the Services is progressing rapidly in British India the Europeanization of the Services must begin in the States, especially those States where the Maharajas do not want to have Parliaments to share or control their power. The States, being backward in education and social life, must have the same chance as British India. The men who made British India what she is may be given a chance in the States.

It may be said that the salaries which the European officers and officials in the States will demand will be higher than the wages paid to the Indians whom they will replace. The answer to that is that the Princes must be prohibited from treating the States as their private property, and must be given a fixed allowance. They must not henceforward abuse public money for private purposes. On a generous scale an allowance must be given to them, which they can spend or hoard according to their tastes and inclinations.[1]

[1] There are various amusing stories current in the State of Hyderabad about the Nizam's ways of hoarding money. The Nizam has the wealth of Midas, being the wealthiest ruler in India. Hyderabad is the largest Indian State, "with an area of 82,700 square miles, with a population of 12,500,000 and a revenue of 6½ crores of rupees, or about £5,000,000."—*States Inquiry Committee Report*, par. 11.

PART III

EVOLUTION OR REVOLUTION?

EXTREMISTS, TRUE AND FALSE—THE VICEROY SEPARATES THE SHEEP FROM THE GOATS

CHAPTER XVI

GANDHI—AND TERROR

THERE are two forces in India, Gandhi—and terror.

Gandhi is known as the *Mahatma* ("High-souled"), a term of reverence usually applied to the great *rishis*, or sages, of India of prehistoric times.

Gandhi earned this title by his plain living and high thinking. He had led a life of perpetual struggle with the white settlers in South Africa. He gave the best part of his life to the vindication of the rights of his countrymen there.

Gandhi is taken by myriads of Indians who know him not at close quarters, but have only had a *darshan* (glimpse) of him from a distance, for a mere saint and no politician. There are greater saints in India than Gandhi, but not more popular or courageous politicians.

A saint does not enter politics, the grave of saintship. Politics are a dirty game—" the last resort of rascals," as one of the Kings of England put it. They are more dirty in a country where political leaders have not acquired the restraint, or the character, or the experience, of those in an advanced country.

If Gandhi is the greatest and the fiercest political leader in India to-day it is because he brings to it the dignity of an Asquith, the noble grandeur of a Gladstone, and the utter recklessness of a Joan of Arc.

Wearing the robes and living the simple life of an Indian saint, he captures the citadel of the people's heart. In India, if one aspires to be a successful political leader, one must be a saint first. Gandhi's saintship is the key to his political leadership.

Gandhi was essentially a moderate in his leader's lifetime, though even then, in his overstrung moments, he used to lisp the language of the extremist. His political *guru* (master) was Gokhale, Morley's friend. Gandhi proved to be the *guru's* despair in the latter's last days. The *guru* forced on his *chela* (follower) a vow of silence for two years when the latter returned home from South Africa with a view to consecrating the rest of his life to the Indian cause.

Gandhi made the most dramatic use of that probationary period. He travelled third class, which the upper middle classes in India avoid. Gandhi comes from an upper middle-class family.

Third-class travelling is most uncomfortable in a hot country of long distances. The compartments are overcrowded. The passengers are packed like sardines. One of the hardy annuals of the Central Legislature is the discomforts of the third-class passengers.

Gandhi took up their cause. He spoke from experience. Newspapers proclaimed how the hero of South Africa would not travel by second or first class, for in India, as on the Continent, you have also a second class.

Gandhi at once became the man of the masses. On the biggest railway platforms crowds used to muster to shout the *jai* (victory) of that strong, silent man from South Africa.

When Gandhi broke his vow of silence Gokhale had gone to the place " where the wicked cease from troubling and the weary are at rest," only to be followed by the biggest leader that modern India and the nationalist movement had produced, Tilak, whom the late Sir Valentine Chirol truly described as " the father of Indian unrest."

Gandhi rallied to his side all the extremist forces ; changed the creed of the Congress from Dominion Home Rule to *Swaraj* ; drove the Moderates and several Nationalists from it—the last of whom to be so driven was Mr M. A. Jinnah, the leader of the Muslim League—and launched a campaign of civil disobedience.

GANDHI—AND TERROR

The Gandhi movement would not have fizzled out but for the timidity of his principal lieutenants, who betrayed him when he was imprisoned. Against his advice they went to the Councils to work the reforms. The most important of them was Patel, to-day the Speaker of India's Parliament.

Speaker Patel told me two years ago, while he was on a pilgrimage to Whitehall and Westminster to learn the ABC of Parliamentary procedure, that Gandhi was not a spent force; that he was "only biding his time"; and that he himself had said so to Lord Birkenhead, the then Secretary of State for India, and to Mr Baldwin, the then Prime Minister. Perhaps Patel was right.

The strength of Gandhi depends on the terrific mass support which he alone among the Indian politicians commands. The lack of character among his followers and their readiness to quarrel among themselves made him sick. The frequent misunderstandings between the Hindus and the Muslims made his heart sink. The refusal of India as a whole to take to the *charka* (spinning-wheel) drove him into the wilderness.

Gandhi has no new philosophy to propound. His plan of campaign is plain and simple—"non-violent non-co-operation." Though he is anxious to avoid violence, the tragedy of his life has been that his movement has always led to violence. He has himself admitted it a hundred times. His "Himalayan blunders," as he loves to call them, only put more faith and more energy in him to overcome them. That he will not overcome them goes without saying. "You can as well speak of vegetarian tigers" is the retort of the revolutionary to Gandhi's propaganda for non-violent non-co-operation.

Gandhi says—and thousands of his followers most sincerely feel likewise—that British rule in India endures not because of the "steel frame" of the European Services, but because of the Indian co-operation. Gandhi is right.

Indians want British rule, and that is why India has British rule. If three hundred millions of people decide not to have the rule of a handful of aliens the decision must hold.

Gandhi's purpose is to overthrow foreign rule without shedding a drop of the adversary's blood ; even though the latter might inflict violence on the national movement, not to answer violence with violence, but to answer it with love.

Gandhi hopes to melt the heart of Britain by suffering. "Suffer," says he, "so that our nation may conquer." Sacrifice, he argues, is native to the land of his birth. Let us then prepare for sacrifices of all kinds ; of our foreign cloth ; foreign ideas ; foreign education ; foreign institutions ; service under a foreign Government ; of personal freedom itself as a penalty for persistent propaganda against co-operation with that Government.

If Gandhi's commandments were obeyed India would be free in no time. But a poor country will always have people to look to the Government for support and maintenance. A Government in every country has resources. The resources of the British Government in India are great. It provides employment for hundreds of thousands of Indians. They are not the people who will follow Gandhi. "Pockets before patriotism" is the motto of the majority of the people all the world over. And India is no exception to the rule.

The revolutionary disapproves of Gandhi's gospel, because it is impractical and its success is impossible unless the whole country were prepared for a general strike lasting for some months. Such a strike cannot be hurriedly brought about. Even if brought about it cannot be kept up for several weeks. Therefore the revolutionary believes in the short cut of secret conspiracies, intimidation of the police, and a general campaign of terrorism against the foreign Government.

Both revolutionaries and Gandhi's followers were preparing for a grim struggle—not against each other, notwithstanding their different methods and conflicting philosophies—against foreign rule. Gandhi himself had proclaimed that he would make the revolutionary gospel of independence his own. It did not occur to that great saint that independence, which is forcible severance of the British connexion, can be attained only by a successful war; through oceans of blood, through fire and sword.

Non-violent non-co-operation, if faithfully carried out, as he would sincerely wish, without creating an atmosphere of bitter race-hatred and violence, could only increase the friendship between Britain and India, inducing the former finally to give the latter equal partnership in the Empire. Non-violent non-co-operation, therefore, was the road to Home Rule, not independence. War was the weapon of those who sought to overthrow British rule.

The revolutionaries naturally felt that Gandhi was only carelessly playing into their hands; they secretly delighted in the thought that the saint would unconsciously prepare the atmosphere for a bloody revolution.

To make matters worse, the Communist, inspired and paid by Moscow, was blowing the bugle of class-war within and war against Imperialism without. On this subject Sir Chimanlal Setalvad, the President of the loyal Moderate Convention, better known as the National Liberal Federation, said: [1]

> I feel bound to draw the serious attention of all who are interested in the welfare and prosperity of this country to the growing menace that is threatening not only the ordered progress of the country, but the very foundation and existence of society and the State. There are indications which cannot be ignored that Communist ideas are being disseminated among the working classes and the ignorant agricultural population with the avowed object of subverting the present

[1] Presidential Address at the eleventh session of the National Liberal Federation, delivered on December 30, 1928.

> structure of society and ownership of property. The repeated and long-continued strikes in important industrial centres which have very nearly ruined the staple industries of the country are engineered not merely for the purpose of redressing the legitimate or supposed grievances and improving the condition of labour, but as part of a plan to break up the present order and structure of society, and are subsidized partly by foreign funds. A party has come into existence which is openly proclaiming revolution and destruction of the present structure of society and ownership of property as its goal.

Who was responsible for the situation? Let Sir Chimanlal Setalvad, himself a member of the Bombay Government till lately, answer:

> Paradoxical as it may seem, it is Government who have by their blundering and hesitating policy at every step created extremism and helped it at every stage to gather greater strength just when it was about to lose ground. Their unwise action in putting the Rowlatt Acts on the Statute Book in defiance of united Indian opinion throughout the country gave birth to civil disobedience. The Punjab Martial Law administration and the horrors for which it was responsible created the cult of non-violent non-co-operation and non-payment of taxes and the obstructive and hostile attitude of the Swarajists in the Legislatures. The Simon Commission muddle of last year brought into existence the party advocating complete independence. Government have always failed to respond adequately and timely to legitimate Indian aspirations as voiced by sane and responsible political sections, and by their hesitation and delay have lost opportunity after opportunity of catching the imagination of the people and securing their contentment. They are so much lost in admiration of what they have done for India and of the efficiency of their administration that they wonder and resent that Indians should be dissatisfied with the present order of things and should demand full self-government.

CHAPTER XVII

THE DIPLOMAT AT WORK

INDIA was in the throes of a revolution. The British *Raj* was faced with a movement the like of which was not known or heard since 1857. Loyal moderates who had always stood for British connexion had gone over to the side of the extremists. A united nation had resolved to rise in revolt. Its representatives had delivered an ultimatum to the British *Raj*. According to the ultimatum, the Indian National Congress would proclaim independence and prepare for civil disobedience and non-payment of taxes unless steps were taken to establish Dominion status in India. The ultimatum was to expire on the midnight of December 31, 1929.[1]

Lord Irwin, the Viceroy of India, was in an extremely difficult position. No Viceroy since the days of Lord Canning had been faced with a crisis of such terrific dimensions and consequence. The only advantage that Lord Irwin had over Lord Canning was this: the former was dealing with English-educated people who were fair in love and fair in war, whereas Lord Canning had to face a surprise mass attack. In 1857 the soldiers and the populace gave no ultimatum to British *Raj*. In 1929 the leaders of the people gave a definite warning in firm, if courteous, language, fully twelve months ahead.

1 "That resolution last year at first stated that, if Dominion *status* was not granted at the end of the year, there would be civil disobedience throughout the country—a very, very grave threat. If I remember aright, it was Mr Gandhi who then appeared on the scene and moderated the severity of this resolution by postponing it for one year, and it is that resolution which is about to be considered in December of this year at Lahore. The object of the resolution is to determine that, unless Dominion *status* is given by the end of that year, civil disobedience with all its consequences will ensue."—The Marquis of Reading, Tuesday, November 5, 1929 (*House of Lords Debates*, vol. 75, p. 383).

The British *Raj* was strong and mighty. It could ignore the ultimatum. The Indian soldiers were contented and loyal. There was no danger of a mutiny in the Army, and therefore no chance of a successful revolution. Lord Irwin could have brushed aside the ultimatum and said: "Do your worst and be prepared for the worst."

Who in India does not remember the exhibition of the might of the British *Raj* in the Punjab ten years ago? Jallianwala Bagh, a public park in Amritsar, was the prolegomena to the inauguration of martial law in the Punjab.[1] It was in that park that unarmed men were shot with the dramatic purpose of creating "an impression"[2] that British *Raj* believed in governing India with the sword.

Not the British people, but the bureaucratic system, was responsible for producing what Lord Curzon described in disgust as "the reeking shambles of Amritsar."[3] Kind words were uttered by the British and Indian Governments to conciliate the Indian people, who—dissatisfied and humiliated—invited Mahatma Gandhi to start a spiritual war against British injustice in India.

All this Lord Irwin knew as the man on the spot. He understood that the British Army and the loyal Indian troops were strong enough to put down any political rising. Even if the worst were to happen the Viceroy was not

[1] *India in 1919*, being the annual report of the Government of India to Parliament.

[2] See evidence of Brigadier-General R. E. Dyer before the Hunter Committee named after Lord Hunter, its Chairman, who began their inquiry into the Punjab disturbances in October 1919.

See also Government of India report, *India in 1920*, Chapter II, pp. 26–50. This official report says:

"In particular, early in the course of the period under review, intense feeling was aroused by the public examination of Brigadier-General R. E. Dyer, who had been responsible for firing upon an assembly at Jallianwala Bagh, in Amritsar, thereby causing the heaviest death-roll in the history of the suppression of the disturbances. The frank-admission of this officer that he had employed measures so drastic with the object of causing moral effect produced a passionate outcry in India which was re-echoed also in Great Britain."

[3] Hansard of 1919 and 1920, relating to Indian debates in Parliament, reveal how high authorities like Lord Curzon deplored the unhappy excesses.

unaware that India—unarmed to-day, thanks to the British policy of keeping her in safe subjugation—could be reconquered with the facility with which Lord Birkenhead would make a speech in the congenial atmosphere of the House of Lords.

The Viceroy of India had before him one of two alternatives: conciliation or repression. He combined both.

A Conservative by upbringing and temperament, he was unwilling wholly to conciliate. A Christian in life and thought, he was opposed to wholesale repression, which meant really martial law and ruthless slaughter of unarmed innocents and rebels, as in the Amritsar crisis. In a crisis it was impossible to distinguish an innocent sympathizer from an active participant in the revolt. The crisis in the Punjab, the dark days of martial law, which rendered the terrific rebellion of Gandhi and his followers inevitable—20,000 of them had to be sent to prison [1]—would have to be repeated on a nation-wide scale if an irreconcilable attitude were taken by the British *Raj*, leaving behind a memory of unforgettable wrongs, unforgivable excesses, and broken pledges.

It did not require much courage to take up an attitude which a Michael O'Dwyer had taken up in the past in the interests of all that was vital to the British people. Sir Michael advised the application of martial law to his province,[2] where, face to face with public uprising, the civil authority was paralysed, as it seemed, at any rate to him, who was considered to be the best judge, being the man on the spot.

It was open, in the name of the British Empire, to the Viceroy of India to hand over the administration of the country to his Excellency the Commander-in-Chief and proclaim martial law in India, even as martial law was proclaimed in Egypt.[3] With the experience, however, of the Punjab a decade ago—and its tragic aftermath which taxed all the resources of the Empire and 'perplexed' one

[1] *Proceedings* of the Indian Legislative Assembly, 1924. [2] *India in 1919*.
[3] *The Egyptian Problem*, by Sir Valentine Chirol.

of the ablest of Englishmen, Lord Reading—it would be no exaggeration to say that the Viceroy of India must be a bold man to have the Punjab experience repeated on a nation-wide scale.

The choice before Lord Irwin was either to stake India upon a hazard as a gambler stakes his heritage on the throw of the dice, or to save this precious jewel of the Crown for the Empire by a stroke of diplomacy. Lord Irwin chose the *rôle* of a diplomat instead of a gambler.

The Indian mind has had a weakness for proclamations. Lord Canning saved India by the Queen's Proclamation in 1857, on which old Indians still look as their Magna Carta. The late Mr Edwin Montagu, who had to face the revolutionary repercussions after the War, lured the right wing of the Congress with a Parliamentary pronouncement. They seceded from the Congress and set up a rival platform known as the National Liberal Federation. They agreed to check the extremist activities by a persistent campaign in the Press and on the platform. They helped the British Government to suppress the Gandhi rebellion and to break up his non-co-operation movement. They did not hesitate to support or initiate the incarceration of their former political colleagues and leaders. They were denounced in savage language by the extremists, who for a while forgot the existence of a foreign Government, but concentrated on ridiculing and destroying their own countrymen who were the willing props of that Government. The wrath of the extremists against the Moderates for putting down a national rebellion against foreign rule could be faced, but the latter could not bear the betrayal by those whom, Wolsey-like, they had served. The Moderates felt that their exclusion from the Simon Commission was an act of gross treachery on Britain's part, for which they were wholly unprepared. It was well-known that Lord Irwin had warned Whitehall that the exclusion of Indians from the Statutory Commission of Inquiry into Indian reforms would be resented in India.

But Lord Birkenhead had turned down Lord Irwin's recommendation, probably with the object of coming to grips with the extremist and the Moderate combined, and reconquering India, instead of following up the weak-kneed policy of Edwin Montagu, which would end in the grant of Dominion status to India, meaning in India's case secession from England, because India was not a Dominion. Indians did not belong to a daughter-race ; the attachment of the Dominions to the mother-country was inconceivable in the case of India. Either India might be governed with a strong hand or lost.

Lord Irwin was not prepared for a bloody reconquest of India. His Christian soul revolted against the very thought of shooting down myriads. Further, as a gentleman, he felt that those who fought for England and helped her in the suppression of the Gandhi revolt deserved better treatment than was accorded to them when they were excluded from the Simon Commission. The appointment of an Indian Central Committee to collaborate with the Simon Commission was made too late. Moreover, it was not the same thing and had not the same power or status as the Simon Commission. The Moderates held aloof, accusing the Viceroy of having let them down. They withdrew all co-operation from the British Royal Commission. They sided with the extremists in their boycott. They sympathized especially with the excesses of the boycott movement, when the boycotters armed themselves with sticks and stones and invited the police *lathi* in return. Their newspapers assailed the Simon Commission with even greater bitterness than the extremist Press. The bomb that burst in India's Parliament early this year delighted their disgusted soul ! They appeared unwilling to oppose even revolutionary outbreaks.[1]

[1] "What was alarming was that responsible opinion did not somehow come forward to reprobate crime, and that is a very unhealthy sign."—The Right Hon. Wedgwood Benn, the Secretary of State for India, in the debate in the House of Commons on Thursday, November 7, 1929 (Hansard, vol. 231, p. 1327).

The extremist is a born boycotter. He will boycott every British Commission, because he has no faith in Britain. Even if Indians had been included in the Simon Commission it would have made no difference to the true extremist. Masqueraders like the Swarajist leader—if not the misled—might have been placated by a mixed commission, but not the left wing of the Congress, the leadership of which is still retained in Bengal.

None was more grateful to Lord Birkenhead for his exclusion of the Moderates from the Simon Commission than the revolutionary patriot who in the fullness of his nationalism throws a bomb or fires a pistol. The revolutionaries thought that at long last their only enemy, the Indian Moderate who was looking forward to the opportunity of serving on the Royal Commission, who always sold his soul for a mess of political pottage, was by the decree of a divine Providence treated with the contempt he deserved. They were amused when the Moderate preached boycott of a Royal Commission. They handed over the platform to the haranguing Moderate. They allowed the Congress right wing to join hands with these disillusioned seceders who had left the Congress and fought the country to please Montagu. They did not mind the constitution-mongering which ended in the production of a so-called All-Parties Demand for substantial Dominion status. Only, they said that that demand should be the irreducible minimum for the Moderates—and for themselves nothing short of independence! The Congress at Calcutta (1928) did not wholly endorse the so-called All-Parties Demand; it was unwilling to lower the flag of independence; it simply supported the impracticable parts of that document which related to universal franchise and adult suffrage. The extremist was clearly scoring. His triumph was complete with the issue of the ultimatum.[1]

[1] "The way to discharge our fiduciary obligations to India is never to yield to threats—never, never!"—Lord Birkenhead in the House of Lords on November 5, 1929 (*House of Lords Debates*, vol. 75, p. 401).

Conservatives and loyal men despaired. The Government of India was preparing for the fray. Its Secretaries, strong men with a will of their own, the best brains from the universities of Britain, were sharpening the sword for the inevitable conflict. They knew they had tremendous support at home. Men like Lord Birkenhead, Mr Winston Churchill, and Earl Winterton, the late Indian Under-Secretary, were not the politicians to be cowed down by the extremists' wild threat.

Alas! the Secretariat hopes were frustrated with the advent of Socialism to power.

Labour stood committed to a sympathetic Indian policy. In his irresponsible and unregenerate days the Labour Premier himself had repudiated in as strong a language as Gandhi—and with close reasoning and searchlight clarity—the present bureaucratic system of Indian administration.[1] Emotional Socialists like Lansbury had proclaimed from a hundred platforms that Britain had no right to impose its rule on an unwilling people.[2] Labour conferences in the past had passed perfervid resolutions on the grant of self-determination to India. It was, therefore, idle to expect a Socialist Government to support a strong campaign of resistance to the Nationalist movement. Uneasy lay Lord Irwin's head.

Lord Irwin had been forced into the morass of isolation from public opinion by Lord Birkenhead's exclusion of Indians from the Commission; Lord Birkenhead was no longer at his back to support a strong policy. He had gone to the City even before his party's fall. Neither was Lord Irwin's party, nor his old chief, whom he loved and who reciprocated his affection,[3] at the helm of affairs.

[1] *Government of India*, by the Right Hon. J. Ramsay MacDonald.

[2] Hansard, November 25, 1927. See Mr Lansbury's speech, in which he says no nation has been born which is fit to govern another.

[3] "If ever the day comes when the party which I lead ceases to attract to itself men of the calibre of Edward Wood (Lord Irwin) then I have finished with my party."—Mr S. Baldwin in the House of Commons on Thursday, November 7, 1929 (Hansard, vol. 231, p. 1306).

Lord Irwin decided to divide the united front in India. A united India England cannot face, except with the sword unsheathed. Every attempt at conciliation must fail before force is resorted to. England's prestige in the East lies not in her rule with brute force, but in her superior tact and capacity to make the Kilkenny cats quarrel among themselves.

Invite them to a conference at Whitehall. The vanity of a vain group of Oriental politicians, *pundits*, and pretenders would be flattered at the thought of sitting at the same table with his Majesty's Ministers discussing the destiny of their race. As they had failed to settle their differences in their round table conferences, so will they fail to adjust them in the eleventh hour in Whitehall. There were conflicting interests which could be adequately represented. The findings of the Simon Commission about a chaos of races and congeries of castes and tongues and mutually antagonistic aspirations could thus be conclusively established. The Empire would be the better for the confounding of the Indian politicians; the King's Government in India stronger by dividing the ranks of the enemy. In the meantime Socialism could be disillusioned by an organized exhibition of Indian incompetence. The absurdity of entertaining the idea of an early grant of Dominion status for any British party could be proved!

Who says that Lord Irwin has betrayed the trust? The ill-informed criticism in a section of the British Press—one organ of which had gone the length of asking for the recall of Lord Irwin and the sending out of Mr Winston Churchill in his place—only shows that even great newspaper editors cannot understand the intricacies and complexities of a situation which the man on the spot, assisted by the most powerful and conservative Secretariat in the world, alone can comprehend.

No wonder the extremists bitterly feel how, with the ruse

of a Proclamation which means nothing tangible and nothing immediate to the advanced school and the offer of a conference, Lord Irwin has succeeded in defeating the purpose of the fire-eating politicians and disillusioning their Socialist supporters here. For the moment, at any rate, Lord Irwin, without firing a single shot or arresting a single leader, has confounded, divided, and demoralized a simple-hearted people of primitive peasants, and isolated the far-sighted, the determined, and the brainy irreconcilables with a view, if necessary, to putting them down.[1] Here is indeed, bewails the revolutionary, Machiavellian statesmanship whose single purpose is to strengthen and consolidate British rule in India with the apparent consent of the governed and postpone the evil day of Dominion status, which in India's case would only mean independence.

[1] "The response favourable to the Viceroy's announcement is wider than might have been expected. The effect of the statement may be summed up as having at a stroke removed the tension from Indian politics and re-introduced a spirit of confidence and trust between Government and governed and *delivered a blow at the Independence movement which has hitherto been gaining daily adherence among Congressmen.*"—Reuter's telegram, quoted with approval by the Secretary of State for India in the House of Commons (Hansard, vol. 231, pp. 1327, 1328).

CHAPTER XVIII

A TRIPARTITE CONFERENCE

SINCE ideas of Home Rule or Dominion status have been brooding over India the Princes and responsible European officials alike have been asking: "Is Home Rule to be granted only to British India or also to the Native States?"

Sir Malcolm Hailey, the ablest administrator in India to-day and the Governor of a big province, called the "United Provinces," which has a population larger than that of Great Britain, asked in one of his masterly orations in the Indian Legislative Assembly (which is India's House of Commons), in his capacity as the Leader of the House and the then Home Member of the Government of India, "Is Dominion self-government to be confined to British India only, or is it to be extended to the Indian States." This question has since caused considerable anxiety among the politicians of British India. They met in conferences and discussed the subject for several months, and came to the conclusion that the Swarajist (Home Rule) Commonwealth of India would embrace both British India and the Native States; that the Commonwealth would take over the present responsibilities and obligations of the British Government of India toward the Indian States; and that when and if any difference between the Swarajist Commonwealth and the Indian States were to arise, in matters such as the interpretation of treaties, engagements, *sunnuds*, or similar other documents, the Governor-General in Council would, with the consent of the State concerned, refer the said matter to the Supreme Court of India-to-be for its final decision.[1]

[1] *Report of the All-Parties Conference* (1928), p. 122.

The Princes, however, did not accept this position. They resented the contemplated interference in their affairs by politicians in British India. They said they did not wish to interfere in British Indian affairs, except when the Congress or other political bodies challenged the supremacy of the Crown. They expected British India's politicians to recognize the time-honoured obligation of mutual abstention.

The Moderates in British India recognized the strength of the Princes' contention. They said that there was a case here for discussion and further exploration, a point of view which seemed to appeal for the moment also to the right wing of the Congress and other constitutionalists outside the Moderate fold.

The All-Parties Conference of 1928 reported with one voice:

> Indeed, if there ever was a case for a Round Table Conference at which a perfect understanding could easily be reached, it was this.[1]

Sir John Simon, the liberal-minded chairman of the Indian Statutory Commission, had publicly applauded the All-Parties Report as an "able" document.[2] The testimony from such a high authority to a rather sloppy publication under a misleading title—because, though called "All-Parties Report," not even all the boycotting parties endorsed it—embarrassed those who had read it. Sober critics who examined it from a distance could not conceal their surprise that Sir John Simon, whom, as the Chairman of the Statutory Commission, the authors of that report had insulted by preaching, planning, and carrying out a programme of unrelenting boycott, should have given a flattering certificate to them and their much-advertised handiwork.[3]

Sir John Simon's *rôle*, however, was not that of a mere

[1] *Report of the All-Parties Conference* (1928), p. 72.
[2] *The Dilemma in India*, p. 229.
[3] *Ibid.*

explorer, but also of an ambassador of peace. He knew that the Indian boycotters, and especially his friend, Motilal Nehru, who had several interviews with him in England in November 1927, had blundered badly in keeping away from the Simon Commission. The very fact that the Indian politicians put their heads together as Pundit Motilal Nehru had anticipated in England, and produced a report for the British Commission's benefit, moved Sir John to give them a kind compliment.

> Kindness is wisdom. There is none in life,
> But needs it and may learn.

Sir John Simon was more than kind when he accepted the advice of the All-Parties Report. He wrote to the Prime Minister, by way of anticipating the conclusions of his own Commission, that it would be necessary to summon a Round Table Conference of the Princes and the politicians, to discuss and to settle the future of India. The following passage from that memorable correspondence may be quoted:

> It seems to us that what would be required would be the setting up of some sort of conference after the Reports of the Statutory Commission and the Indian Central Committee have been made, considered and published, and their work has been completed, and that in this conference his Majesty's Government would meet both representatives of British India and representatives of the States (not necessarily always together) for the purpose of seeking the greatest possible measure of agreement for the final proposals which it would be later the duty of his Majesty's Government to submit to Parliament.[1]

The Prime Minister promptly accepted the advice of the Chairman of the Statutory Commission regarding the

[1] Letter of Sir John Simon, chairman of the Indian Statutory Commission to the Prime Minister, dated October 16, 1929. The India Office issued the correspondence between Sir John Simon and the Prime Minister on the night of October 30, which appeared in *The Times* and other morning papers in London on October 31, 1929.

summoning of a Round Table Conference in Downing Street, whose purpose, he interpreted with the authority attaching to his position, was to bring "the whole problem under comprehensive review." The Prime Minister further emphasized that "His Majesty's Government are also greatly concerned to find means by which they may approach the treatment of the broad question of British Indian Constitutional advance in co-operation with all those who can speak authoritatively for British Indian political opinion." The Prime Minister therefore supported the adoption of procedure that will permit the free representation of all points of view.

Close on the publication of this interesting correspondence went a thrilling "message" to India from the Indian Member in the British Cabinet, as Mr George Lansbury is called. India has been for long years Mr Lansbury's love. Mr Lansbury has been for the last few months the moving spirit behind the scenes in Whitehall leading up to the announcement of a new policy, the inauguration of a new era. Mr Lansbury told me two years ago that Lord Birkenhead had committed a great blunder in excluding Indians from the Statutory Commission. Mr Lansbury was principally responsible for securing for the Indian Central Committee the status and authority to sit with the Simon Commission throughout the entire stage of inquiry and submit a separate report. Mr Lansbury, who accompanied Mr Snowden and Mr MacDonald, had more interviews than one with Lord Birkenhead, the then Secretary of State, to get the evil effect of the exclusion of Indians from the Royal Commission mitigated by expanding the status and function of the Central Committee. This wise policy weaned from the boycotters men of the eminence of Sir Chettur Sankaran Nair and Sir Hari Singh, who collaborated and co-operated with the British Commission, but still men of the eminence of Sir Chimanlal Setalvad and Sir Sivaswamy Iyer, both of them once members of the Bombay and Madras Governments, and other leaders of Liberal and Nationalist Parties, like Mrs Besant, remained unsatisfied.

Hence the Conservative Viceroy's Proclamation and Mr Lansbury's message explaining it.

Lord Birkenhead was furious when he read in the papers that Mr Lansbury had issued an astounding message to the Indian people on their inalienable right to self-government.

Thanks to the courtesy of Parliament to the members of the Empire Parliamentary Association, I, who stood below the bar of the House of Lords listening to the speech of Lord Birkenhead, was convinced that his Lordship understood the meaning of the new move and the leading spirit in Whitehall behind the Indian Home Rule Movement.[1] He was none other than that grey-haired Socialist, George Lansbury, who is worshipped in India as a second Gandhi.

Lord Birkenhead was answered by his Majesty's Secretary of State for India, who said in his spirited speech in the House of Commons that Mr Lansbury's message to India was the keynote of the Government's policy.[2] The emotional Mr Lansbury—as I could see from my place in the Dominions Gallery—was moved at the rich tribute of a loyal colleague, loyalty being so rare a thing in politics.

[1] "Mr Lansbury has sent his love to the peoples of India; three hundred and forty millions of them, so that each particular recipient is likely to obtain a fragmentary portion. It is rather like the pieces of a bridal cake. . . . Why is Mr Lansbury distributing his love all over India?"—Lord Birkenhead (*House of Lords Debates*, vol. 75, pp. 403, 404).

[2] "A good deal of jocularity has been indulged in at the expense of the message of my Right Honourable friend the First Commissioner of Works. I wonder if everybody had read that message. Lord Birkenhead, who is an expert in taste, saw fit to joke at the terms of the message. Well, my Right Honourable friend the First Commissioner has an expansive manner—there is no doubt about that—but when he spoke about 'love,' I will say 'love' that is 'goodwill' is the keynote of British policy. There has been an effort made to make the Indian people realize the position which they occupy in the British Commonwealth, to give them an assurance of equality."—Mr Wedgwood Benn, Secretary of State for India, in the Commons (Hansard, vol. 231, pp. 1328, 1329).

A TRIPARTITE CONFERENCE

Amid scenes of animation, amid much feeling in both Houses, England stands definitely committed to the pledge of Dominion status to India as a whole, that "Greater India," as Lord Irwin announced in his Viceregal Proclamation,[1] issued with the approval and authority of his Majesty's Government in Great Britain.

[1] Published in a *Gazette of India Extraordinary* on the night of October 31.

CHAPTER XIX

THE VICEROY'S PROCLAMATION—AND AFTER

As Lord Canning proclaimed to India in another century on the eve of a great mutiny the intention and purpose of the Queen of England, even so Lord Irwin proclaimed on the morn of a threatened rebellion his Majesty's pledge and programme in regard to India's fate and future.

The Queen's pledge was a balm to the wounds of the Indian people. The Viceregal Proclamation, *bearing the stamp of authority of his Majesty's Government*, was an escape, however temporary, from the casualties inevitable to war. Carrying as the Proclamation did the authority of a Government presided over by a Prime Minister, himself a pacifist during the last war, who had just returned from a mission of peace from the transatlantic continent, it had a significance which was appreciated even by men apparently so irreconcilable as Gandhi, also a pacifist.

What did the Viceroy say? Did he depart from Parliament's pledge to India embodied in the preamble to the Government of India Act?

In his Proclamation [1] to the Indian people his Majesty's Viceroy and Governor-General of India conveyed to those whom he meant to comfort the impression of his contact with the Socialist Government in Great Britain during his holiday at Home; how he communicated to the latter his own "anxieties" in regard to India, which was on the verge of a veritable revolution under the leadership of Balraj, who, by the way, was responsible for the bombs that burst in India's Parliament, as if to inform Sir John

[1] Published in a *Gazette of India Extraordinary* and in London on November 1, 1929.

Simon, seated in the gallery, of "India's feelings and aspirations," to borrow the language of the Viceroy's Proclamation; and how his Majesty's Government were animated by "a generous and sincere desire" to placate political India.

The Viceroy had not faltered in his belief—notwithstanding the ocean of "misunderstandings" which divided him from the political leaders—that behind all the unrest there lay the vast masses of people "fundamentally loyal to the King-Emperor"—a loyalty which stood in danger of being undermined by the agitator, if he was not conciliated. He was satisfied at the same time that England, which appreciated this loyalty, was always willing to reward it by persisting in its policy of fulfilling the pledges given to India from time to time. It was with a desire "to redeem to the full the pledges she has given for India's future"[1] that Lord Irwin made the Proclamation on behalf of his Majesty's Government.

The most striking feature of the new pledge to which the Viceroy committed his Majesty's Government and the Government of India was its promise of Dominion status.

Dominion status for the whole of India was never publicly promised before. The goal of Britain in India was confined only to British India and not to the Indian States. For the first time, definitely and irrevocably, the Viceroy committed England to the policy of promoting Dominion status, not for British India alone, as intended by the authors of the Montagu-Chelmsford Report and approved by Parliament, but also for the Indian States, or, more correctly, for both combined—"the Greater India," as he termed it.

The Viceroy's words, hailed as a Magna Carta by the

[1] "We have promised India in our declaration responsible government. Do we mean it or do we not? I will say at once that all classes in this country are agreed that the pledge shall be honoured in the letter and in the spirit."—Mr S. Baldwin in the Indian Debate on November 7, 1929, in the House of Commons (Hansard, p. 1310).

millions of India, must be placed on record, because the wars of the future will be based on that pledge, if it is not redeemed in the spirit, remembering the circumstances in which it was given:

> I am authorized on behalf of his Majesty's Government to state clearly that *the natural issue* of India's constitutional progress is the attainment of Dominion status.

A neater or a bolder promise was never given. For the fulfilment of the pledge, alike in point of time and the measure of advance, the Viceroy tenaciously clung to the Montagu programme, since incorporated in the preamble of the Government of India Act. But as a striking enunciation of Britain's policy in India it was definitely an improvement on Mr Montagu's rather vague declaration of August 1917.

Incidentally, Lord Irwin's new pledge drove a nail into the coffin of the familiar Reading policy, to wreck which Mahatma Gandhi had waged an uncompromising war. That policy was no more and no less than that of his predecessor, Lord Chelmsford, the Viceroy who was associated with Edwin Montagu's experiments in democracy. Neither Lord Reading nor his predecessor had conceded that al. India was to be endowed, even in the distant future, with Dominion status. All that they had believed in was the grant of Dominion status to British India, a policy which had nothing whatever to do with the Indian States.

To the credit of Lord Irwin be it said that he induced the Socialist Government to include in Mr Montagu's dream and the Parliament's pledge British India and the Indian States put together. Small wonder that Lord Reading was hurt.[1] Small wonder that this Liberal Imperialist felt that Lord Irwin had squandered his legacy.

[1] Read Lord Reading's letter to the Secretary of State for India, which he read out in his speech in the House of Lords (November 5, 1929) while explaining his censure motion on the approval of the Viceroy's Proclamation by the British Government (*House of Lords Debates*, vol. 75, pp. 378, 379).

Small wonder that he assailed his successor's policy with a ruthlessness the justification for which was only the critic's enthusiasm for the Empire's future. Lord Irwin, however, was concerned more with the present !

India's future as interpreted by the Viceroy and his Majesty's Government, and approved by the Conservative and the Liberal Parties, who dared not press a censure motion to a division and seek the verdict of a philanthropic British electorate on the Indian issue, is the simultaneous growth of responsible government in British India and the Indian States, culminating in the securing of Dominion status.

It was not a pious repetition of an ancient idea propounded by Macaulay, who dreamt of an English-educated India aspiring for Anglo-Saxon institutions. It was not a half-hearted pursuit of a feeble policy enunciated by Morley of administration by consultation through advisory Councils, with an elected Opposition and a permanent government by the Civil Services. Nor was it the nominal reiteration of the Montagu pledge, which only vaguely spoke of responsible government as an ultimate goal for Pan-India. Lord Irwin's was a clear and unequivocal Proclamation, a solemn pledge to promote Dominion status, which was the burning "issue" arising from the constitutional progress attained by India. Above all, the Proclamation was a recognition of the right of Indians to self-determination, because the Viceroy included in the Proclamation not only the enunciation of a policy, the declaration of the objective, but also the way in which that policy was to be enforced, the method by which that objective was to be attained. Indian leaders were to be invited to Whitehall, even as Irish leaders were invited by the Coalition Government, to a conference which could—*given wisdom and tolerance on both sides*—settle the Indian problem, or, at any rate, pave the way for a reasonable settlement.

This was certainly a vigorous move toward the fulfilment of Britain's obligations and India's aspirations. That a

Conservative Viceroy should have initiated that step reveals as by a flash that Conservatism is still a living force, and it will conserve in the future, as it has preserved in the past, all that is vital and real to the Empire.

India is the Empire's proudest possession. Take away India and the British Empire is robbed of its pride and glory. Lord Irwin has saved India for the Empire, not as Ireland was saved by the grant of partial Dominion status, but by a promise that full Dominion status *in the fullness of time* for the whole of India was the undoubted and undeniable goal, and early steps would be taken for the establishment of self-government in British India, after discussing its relations with the Indian States, in a conference of the Princes and the people.

The question of immediate Dominion status for Pan-India does not arise. All that is asked for by responsible Indians is responsible government for British India as distinguished from the Indian States, though even in this respect extremist masqueraders like Pundit Motilal Nehru—the leader of the Swaraj party, who preaches independence and plans co-operation, and ends by spoiling the cause alike of the co-operator and the non-co-operator—want nothing more than a Provincial Home Rule and some responsibility in the Central Government, leaving the Political and Foreign Department (which deals with the Indian States and Foreign Affairs) and the Army in the control of the Government of India, responsible, as hitherto, to Great Britain and not to the Indian people.

That is all that Indians of the most pretentious, ferocious type like Pundit Motilal Nehru mean by Home Rule. The Chairman of the Congress, Jawaharlal Nehru, whom misguided critics take for a Communist, though he has been resisting the affiliation of the Indian National Congress to the Third International of Moscow, rushed to welcome Lord Irwin's Proclamation, to the surprise of his adherents, who had imagined that he was going to be the commander-in-chief of the Indian Army of the National Congress, which was to have declared war on the midnight of December 31, 1929, if England did not respond to the Congress ultimatum to establish Dominion status on the morning of January 1, 1930 ! ! !

Lord Irwin has undertaken no such responsibility. His pledge did not concede that Dominion status would be established in the small hours of January 1, 1930, for the whole of India or even for British India alone. His pledge denies any such presumption by the extremist imposters of India, just as it repudiates the gospel of those reactionaries in England who say India cannot be fit for Dominion status. Had the Chairman of the Lahore Congress any sincerity or honesty of purpose he either would not have agreed to welcome the Viceregal Proclamation and recognize its undoubted "sincerity," or, having done so, would not have ventured to go back on his signature like a petty political trickster, turning his wrath against the Viceroy. This is humbugging pure and simple. The truth is that the young Nehru is a log of wood in a sea of chance.

The talk of war on the British *Raj*, which had been indulged in by the tempestuous patriots, has ended. Lord Irwin has killed that cry by a declaration of policy. The Congress leaders who yesterday had falsely accused Lord Irwin in the height of their power of "breach of faith" have to-day published a manifesto applauding his "sincerity" and asking for predominant representation for themselves at the forthcoming conference in London! The Swarajist leader who had himself stood as a candidate for the representation of the Indian Parliamentarians at an Imperial function in Canada—the Empire Parliamentary Conference of two years ago—began dreaming dreams of leading the Indian deputation to England and dining with the Prime Minister in Whitehall. He waited on the Viceroy on Christmas Eve!

The Independence movement was exposed to contempt.

Its own leader, Mr Srinivasa Iyengar, had already resigned his position, for the frequent shock of betrayal by friends and colleagues was too much for him. "The Congress has become a Moderate show," he exclaimed in anguish, and broke down in tears. Young Nehru, the seeming fanatic of the Independence School, who is also the Chairman of the Indian National Congress this year and the Trade Union Congress, stood discredited. Realizing that followers and leaders alike of his school look upon his going over to the Government side and co-operating with the Viceroy and the British Government with a view to discussing the future of India and the introduction of reforms, which at best can only be a substantial stage in the development of Dominion status, leave alone "independence," as an unexpected betrayal, the Young Nehru prepared a strong speech for the Lahore Congress in Christmas week restating his original position, going back on his own signature welcoming the Viceroy's proclamation, and pretending that he was "cheated." This was anticipated by so shrewd an observer as Lord Birkenhead.[1] The purpose of the Congress Chairman's facing both ways is only to cheat his own followers, who cannot always be hoodwinked.

Lord Irwin's victory, however, is complete. If the Congress will declare independence it will only make a laughing-stock of itself, because the Moderates will fight it and crush it with Government support, as they fought and crushed the non-co-operation movement. If, on the other hand, the Congress will not declare independence then the national flag will be definitely lowered, and none dare talk glibly of independence in the future, lest the Government should treat it as sedition or treason.[2] It would have been impossible without facing a prosecution to talk of independence twenty years ago. Those who preached inde-

[1] Speech in the House of Lords on Tuesday, November 5, 1929 (*House of Lords Debates*, vol. 75, No. 13, p. 403).

[2] These chapters were written before the Congress. I leave them as they are. My anticipation has proved wholly correct.

pendence, like Arabinda Ghose and Tilak, had to face prosecution and imprisonment. The cry of independence has been raised recently by a thousand tongues. The Government dared not prosecute the independence-preachers, because their number was legion. Even the Moderates who were losing faith in Britain's sense of fair play threatened to preach independence ! All that is now past history. After Lord Irwin's pledge the independence people will have no greater enemies to face than the Moderates, whose reputation has been considerably increased by the All-Parties Report, of which they are the authors.

An astute extremist warned Nehru in the beginning, when he was unconsciously rehabilit..ting the position of the Moderates by asking them to draft the National demands embodied in the All-Parties Report. " To flirt with the Moderates," said this young man, " is like embracing a crocodile."

The Moderates tempted the Congress with an all-party constitution, rehabilitated their position, and prepared for the destruction of the Congress itself, if only the Government would " appease " them. If not, woe to the Government, because they would egg on the extremists to create " a civil disturbance ! " [1]

What if Lord Irwin has paid the price for winning the Moderate back to the bureaucratic fold ? The price from the British point of view was worth paying. According to Clive, Indians have to be fought with the help of Indians themselves. Lord Irwin proposes to keep what Lord Clive had won by following his example. He has made the position of the Congress leaders ridiculous, their retreat inevitable. But if they do not retreat theirs will be like the historic, patriotic, Balaclava Charge !

[1] " Why was this particular moment selected for their appeasement ? . . . It was because a grave threat had been made subversive of civil government in India. It was because, supported by the names of men of great political position in India, we were menaced at the end of the year with a campaign of civil disturbance."—Lord Birkenhead in the House of Lords on November 5, 1929 (*House of Lords Debates*, vol. 75, p. 401).

CHAPTER XX

THE THREATENED REVOLT

IF Dominion status is not granted early enough, can India revolt successfully? Will she repeat her adventure of 1920 and 1921, when Gandhi launched his Home Rule Campaign?

That the Gandhi movement was powerful even Lord Reading has not denied, in his numerous speeches on India. In fact, Lord Reading's admirers have been giving him credit for having ridden the storm.

But how did he ride the storm? Was it really Lord Reading who put down the Gandhi rebellion?

No, it was not Lord Reading, but Gandhi's own folly in having boycotted the visit of the Prince of Wales.

Lord Reading, finding himself in a hopeless position, imagined that as the Gandhi war had for its objective not independence, but Dominion Home Rule, if his Excellency were to invite the Prince of Wales to visit India Gandhi would suspend his movement.

It was a silly blunder for any politician to drag the Royal House of Windsor into the political whirlpool. When India was seething with discontent it was the most improper thing for Lord Reading to have exposed our future ruler, the Prince of Wales, to the risk of a boycott.[1]

Lord Reading was, of course, making a bold experiment. If the visit of the Prince of Wales were to succeed, Indian loyalty would have been demonstrated to the world, and

[1] Sir Reginald Craddock describes, in his recent book, the organization of "a general boycott of receptions in honour of the Prince of Wales," the unfortunate disturbances in Bombay "on the day of the Prince's arrival," and "the paralysis of business in Calcutta."—*The Dilemma in India*, p. 196 (Constable, 1929).

Lord Reading would have covered himself with credit. Unfortunately, however, Lord Reading had not counted the terrible consequence to India and the Empire of the failure of his experiment.

All patriotic and loyal Indians have deeply deplored that a gifted Viceroy should have been so tactless as to invite the Prince of Wales to India to combat the Home Rule Movement. Had Lord Reading's purpose been clear to Britain it would not have agreed to send out our popular Prince on such a perilous adventure. At the eleventh hour Lord Reading publicly invited Gandhi to a Round Table Conference in Calcutta to call off the boycott of the royal messenger of peace.

Gandhi bitterly retorted that he wanted a change of heart, and that he had repeatedly warned the Viceroy in his weekly journal, *Young India*, and in his speeches, not to invite the Prince at such a crisis, when India was at war, peaceful though it was, with England ; that India would treat such an invitation as an exploitation by the Viceroy of the high esteem in which the Royal House of Windsor and India's future Emperor were held ; that the National Congress would be compelled to declare a boycott of the receptions to the Prince, and observe mourning wherever his Royal Highness went to impress their future Emperor that his father's subjects were not happy. Here it must be said that both Mahatma Gandhi and Lord Reading were wrong. Gandhi should not have boycotted his Royal Highness, knowing right well that the Royal House was above politics. At the same time, Lord Reading, should not have exploited the popularity of the Prince of Wales to rehabilitate his own position in the public eye. Gandhi apologetically wrote that he meant no insult to the Prince, who was the future ruler of India ; that he still believed in Dominion status ; but that he would not allow the trick of Lord Reading's to go unchallenged, even at the risk of being misunderstood.

Had only Gandhi the wisdom of a diplomat, had he suspended his boycott during the Prince's tour, even the Moderate forces would have rallied to his side.

Either way Lord Reading would have lost. Neither Gandhi's wisdom nor folly could have helped him. It is now universally admitted that Lord Reading made an extraordinary blunder in exposing loyal Indians to witness the humiliation of boycott by the extremist of their beloved Prince. Though it brought down on Gandhi the wrath of the Liberals and the Moderates and the terrible vendetta of Lord Reading's own Government, the fact remains that a Jewish Viceroy had sown the dragon's teeth of independence. Gandhi emerged from prison only to see his forces divided into two—those who stood out for Home Rule and those who believed in the violent overthrow of the British *Raj* and the cutting off of all connexions with England.

The Home Rulers, under the leadership of Patel, turned their activities to the Legislatures, which Gandhi had boycotted. Patel is not a man of much physical or moral courage. His bewildered followers thought that if Gandhi could be imprisoned it would not take long for Patel also to be locked up. Discretion is the better part of valour! They decided to capture the Councils with a view to obstructing the Government, for which job Patel was quite good. They also elected Patel as the Speaker of the Assembly, for from the Speaker's chair it would be possible to embarrass the Government, if only one had the boldness—and a clear conscience in the matter—to use a judicial position for a patriotic purpose. Speaker Patel believes in the motto, "The end justifies the means." The end was to embarrass the Government. There was nothing wrong if the Speakership could serve an end for so patriotic a purpose—to hasten the nation's deliverance.

Thus Lord Irwin had a worse situation to face than Lord Reading. The Legislatures, including the Speaker of India's Parliament, were against the Viceroy, and doing everything in their power to embarrass and obstruct the Government. Out in the country a revolutionary movement had been launched which was a challenge to the British supremacy in India.

Lord Reading did not have an inconvenient Legislature. Its members were good boys. Gandhi and his followers had boycotted themselves from the Legislatures on the ground that the Montagu reforms were tainted by the shooting of unarmed people in Amritsar. And those who throve on Gandhi's boycott were loyal Moderates who believed in Britain's generosity.

Notwithstanding the fact that the Legislatures of the land stood solidly by his Lordship, and the Liberal and Moderate Press was with one voice supporting the Government, Lord Reading, to save his face and improve India's loyalty, felt it necessary to invite the Prince of Wales—a policy which both British and Indian opinion has since strongly and rightly disapproved.

Now imagine the impossible circumstances which enveloped Lord Reading's successor. The Moderates and Liberals, in Press and on platform, were savagely assailing the *bona fides* of the British Government, because for the first time in India's history Indians were excluded from a Royal Commission of Inquiry. Lord Irwin had advised Lord Birkenhead not to exclude those Indians who, against Gandhi and the Congress, incurring much public obloquy, had worked the reforms. But the Conservative Secretary of State, ignorant of the state of affairs in India, had turned down the recommendation of the man on the spot, who was himself a great Conservative and his former colleague in the Cabinet.

Lord Irwin loyally carried out Lord Birkenhead's wish, but the result was disastrous. The Simon Commission was assailed with stones and sticks and bombs. British prestige had sunk to the zero-point. Taking advantage of the situation, the extremists had decided to embark on a campaign of civil disobedience. The Moderates were in sympathy with Gandhi and the Congress, and would have entered the whirlpool of revolution themselves.

A crisis a hundred times more serious than the one which faced Lord Reading, obstruction in the Legislatures, boycott out in the open, and the revolutionary emerging from underground with his bomb and pistol, had threatened the British Empire. Lord Irwin decided to break up the movement of independence. He had given repeated warnings to that effect in the past.

There were two or three ways open to the Governor-General of re-establishing British prestige. First, to invite a member of the Royal House to inspire the loyalists; or, secondly, to adopt the Punjab methods of Sir Michael O'Dwyer, including the declaration of martial law and its attendant excesses; or, thirdly, to divide the forces, as Lord Morley did nearly a quarter of a century ago, when the storm was brewing in Bengal, by rallying the Moderates and harrying the extremists.

Lord Irwin, therefore, sent for the Moderate leaders and asked them what they wanted. His Excellency particularly took into his confidence Sir Chimanlal Setalvad, the leader of the All-India Liberal Party, formerly a member of the Bombay Government—when Lord Lloyd was the Governor—which put Gandhi in prison and extinguished the non-co-operation movement.

Sir Chimanlal promised to support the Viceroy, but urged in the first place that his Excellency should make an unambiguous proclamation about the immediate objective of Dominion status; secondly, that a Round Table Conference should be convened in Whitehall to repair the blunder committed by Lord Birkenhead, on the advice of Lord Reading, of excluding the Liberals and Moderates from the Simon Commission; and, thirdly, that a general amnesty should be proclaimed for the political prisoners.

An immediate grant of Dominion status was not in the Viceroy's power. The Montagu policy must prevail until the Montagu Reforms Act was altered. But a general proclamation about Dominion status, being the "natural issue" of the Montagu reforms, could be made by way of explanation and elucidation of a policy which was misunderstood by India because misinterpreted by some tactless officials. Further, a Round Table Conference could be convened—that was the "natural issue" arising from the publication of the Simon and States Inquiry Committee Report—in Whitehall to save the faces of the Moderate and Liberal politicians. Gandhi and the Congress could also be invited. If they accepted the invitation so much the better. If they did not that was also well, because Gandhi and the Congress could be isolated, and the support of all the moderate and independent elements could be secured to attack and annihilate the independence movement.

Lord Irwin, however, could not agree to the proclamation of a general amnesty, as the object of the Round Table Conference was not to draw up a scheme of Dominion Home Rule. It was meant as a sop to the Moderates.

Accordingly, after consulting the Secretary of State, Lord Irwin, as we have seen, issued a proclamation in which he clarified the pledge of Dominion status, implicit in Mr Montagu's pronouncement of 1917, and announced the summoning of a Round Table Conference of the representatives of the British Government, of the Princes, and of the people of British India. This proclamation won the Moderates again to the side of Lord Irwin. It has also, strangely enough, received the suspicious support of fanatics like the Nehrus, who, it is well known, are malicious, do not want to settle matters, and like to keep the Indian unrest going, lest they should find their professional leadership and political occupation gone.

Only one honest leader of Young India, Mr Subosh Bose

of Bengal, on whom the mantle of C. R. Das has fallen, courted isolation and frankly declined to read into the Viceregal Proclamation a meaning which it did not contain. The position, said Mr Bose, remained unchanged, alike in regard to the goal and the time in which the goal was to be reached. Subsequent debates in the House of Lords and Commons and the correspondence exchanged by the Leader of the Opposition and the Prime Minister proved that Bose was right. Bose declined to welcome the Viceroy's Proclamation, rejected the offer of a Round Table Conference, and resolved to persuade the Congress to his way of thinking.

The Congress leaders who conditionally accepted the offer of a Round Table Conference had done so on the pretext that the Conference was going to implement the grant of Dominion status, whereas it was mainly going to discuss the recommendations of the Simon Commission, which they had boycotted. Either, therefore, the Conference will be held without the Congress Leaders, or they will come to England, place their demands for Home Rule before his Majesty's Government, which obviously the latter cannot grant, because, in the first place, they do not believe that India is to-day fit for Home Rule; secondly, his Majesty's Opposition, both Liberal and Conservative, are decidedly opposed to the grant of immediate Home Rule to India, and would throw out the Labour Government on the issue of Indian Home Rule, a contingency for which, as more Socialist Ministers than one have told me—including the Right Hon. George Lansbury—the Labour Government are not prepared.

The future alone can say whether the Proclamation of Lord Irwin, followed by the Round Table Conference, will bring about peace or a situation approaching war. War or peace, Lord Irwin has made the path easy for the present by weaning the Moderates from the extremists.

The future really depends on the decisions of the Round Table Conference and the recommendations of the Simon

Commission. If a substantial measure of self-government is given the Moderates will agree to work the reforms. The extremists will either agree to make the task of the Moderates easy by boycotting the reforms, preaching revolution, and cheerfully courting imprisonment, or they will themselves capture the place of power.

The extremist decision will largely depend on the measure of self-government conceded. For instance, if complete autonomy is granted in the provinces the extremists will agree to run the provincial administration, just as they are running at present the municipalities and District Boards. Even in the height of the non-co-operation movement of 1920–21 Gandhi advised his followers not to boycott the municipalities and District Boards because they had self-government in the local bodies. Already the talented President of the All-India Independence League, Mr S. Srinivasa Iyengar, who is also the leader of the left wing of the Congress, and the Deputy Leader of the Swaraj Party, has publicly proclaimed that the moment provincial autonomy is granted to his province of Madras he will call upon his party to accept office and form the Government, while no doubt the struggle will continue in spheres in which the principle of self-government is not applied.

The present campaign of independence is only a clever move on the part of Jawaharlal Nehru, the Lahore Congress Chairman, to increase his influence and popularity, so that when autonomy is granted to the United Provinces, where he has his residence, he will, with a large party behind him, become the Prime Minister and the Leader of the House.

Most of these men who are preaching war are really thinking of office and power. They are now counting the chickens of the Simon Commission. They will make a big show of boycott when the Reforms Bill is discussed in Parliament, with the object of 'dishing' the Moderates and other co-operators. And then they will rush to the Councils to secure every available office—Ministership, Speakership,

Secretaryship, etc. These false extremists do not want Home Rule for India. They only want jobs.

Not so the revolutionary—with his burning sincerity—who would continue to struggle for his country's freedom.

The Government's policy will be to weaken the revolutionary by widening the bounds of freedom.

The quicker the pace of evolution the slower the march of revolution. The larger the measure of reforms the less the strength of the extremists.

CHAPTER XXI

INDIAN LEADERSHIP UNMASKED !

ONE of the benefits of British rule in India is the production of a new class of people known as the English-educated middle classes. Yet, as an English observer has said, " India is to all intents and purposes almost as much a foreign country to-day as when the British first began to take possession," because the English-educated classes have become " strongly anti-English." [1] But there is a better way of putting it ; they have imbibed the Anglo-Saxon spirit, and aspire for Anglo-Saxon institutions.

The educated classes are spoken of as "a drop in the ocean," [2] or as aspiring to form a brown bureaucracy in the place of a white one. This cannot be lightly denied, but is defended by them on the ground that an indigenous bureaucracy is better than an alien one.

The politicians are a timid lot. The most unscrupulous and aggressive of them becomes the leader, even though he may lack the moral courage in a crisis of his own creation.

This takes us to the bomb that burst in India's Parliament early this year. To maintain his reputation for fireworks as the Congress President, Pundit Motilal Nehru, who leads Indian politics, embarked on a violent obstruction. He stopped the Finance Member from speaking. Patel, the Speaker, openly sided with the Swarajists, and ruled out the anti-Bolshevik Bill. The Viceroy had to enforce it over the head of the Legislature by issuing an ordinance. The Revolutionary came to the rescue of Patel and Pundit alike. He decided to annihilate the entire official block in the

[1] *Indian Jottings*, by Edward F. Elwin, pp. 151, 152.
[2] *Courts and Camps in India*, by Yvonne FitzRoy, p. 234.

Legislative Assembly, and threw two bombs, which fortunately killed nobody. Pundit and Patel squealed! The younger Nehru—whom ill-informed rumour has declared to be a Soviet agent and panic-stricken people take for a full-blooded revolutionary—more in panic than with sincerity, denounced the young men as lunatics and their action as the work of lunatics! The young men in their statement in the court parenthetically retorted that they were not lunatics, but believed in using all weapons to wrest freedom from alien yoke, and they who called them lunatics were cowards. Young Nehru then, by way of repentance, applauded their courage and spirit of self-abnegation!

The Nehrus have always been like the proverbial animal in the lion's skin. They flirt with the revolutionary to secure leadership. No wonder they are not respected in Bengal, the home and hearth of revolutionary nationalism, where spurious Moscow politics are always ridiculed. "Vodka has gone to his head," exclaimed one of the Swarajist organs of Bengal while speaking of the young Nehru's misguided Russian politics.[1]

Bengal is still the leader of the Indian revolt. It will not in a hurry accept outside leadership unless satisfied alike of its incorruptibility and superiority. The only occasion when Bengal owed temporary allegiance to a foreigner was in 1920, when Bengal's leader, the late C. R. Das—the greatest man of his day—accepted the leadership of the saint of Guzerat, Gandhi, even though Das differed from Gandhi's philosophy.

Das was a man of heroic mould. When he passed away the whole of India mourned his loss. There were lengthy paragraphs in his praise even in the British and American newspapers. High officials from the Viceroy downward communicated to his widow their deep sympathy. Das was a brave opponent. Britain and Britishers in India admire an honourable and heroic foe, however uncompromising.

[1] *The Fascination of Russia*, by Pundit Jawaharlal Nehru, M.A. (Cantab.) (an Indian publication).

The utter selflessness of Das captured the imagination of young India. When he unfurled the banner of revolt against the British *Raj* in Bengal his wife and sister and his only son, who is now no more, were in the vanguard of the movement. The son went to prison before any other young man of Bengal. When the young man returned from prison Das was planning another attack, known as the Tarakeswar front. Before appealing for volunteers Das again sent his only son first to the battlefield.

His lieutenants pleaded with him, but he said, "Why should I ask some one else's son to enrol in the list if my son will not be the first to go to the front?" Such a man was bound to lead. Speeches of Lord Birkenhead in the House of Lords, and writings of Lord Ronaldshay, ex-Governor of Bengal, reveal the respect in which even they held C. R. Das, the most difficult of their opponents. C. R. Das's flaming patriotism and terrific leadership made Lord Reading exclaim in one of his Viceregal speeches: "I am puzzled and perplexed."

The way in which Das sent his son first to the Swarajist battle-front struck the imagination of the people. Contrast with it the scene in Allahabad at the same time, and you get an idea at once of the lack of that quality of daring and sacrifice in the present national leadership. His secretary then and successor after his death to Congress Party leadership, Motilal Nehru, and his family were in tears when news reached them of the impending arrest of their only son, Jawaharlal Nehru, simultaneously with the humble publisher of a local Congress daily newspaper, *The Independent*. Fortunately intervention came from Pundit Madan Mohan Malaviya, a schoolmate of Motilal Nehru's. Pundit Malaviya is a loyal leader of the Hindus, a constant visitor to Government Houses, and the Vice-Chancellor of the Hindu university. Pundit Madan Mohan went to Government House, saw Sir Harcourt Butler, the then Governor of the United Provinces, and the Maharaja of Mahmudabad, the

Home Member, and requested them not to arrest Nehru's only son. The result was that Nehru's only son and heir was saved, and the publisher of *The Independent* was sacrificed! The latter was proceeded against and given a year's rigorous imprisonment.

The son could not be saved from prison for long, nor even the father. When they gave a demonstration of their petulance and disloyalty during the visit of the Prince of Wales, and preached social boycott[1]—which loyal India deplored and Liberal politicians considered as an act of madness—and indulged in disobedience of certain laws, they were arrested and imprisoned.

Six months' course in the U.P. gaol broke the spirit of the Swarajist leader. He abandoned non-co-operation, entered the Legislative Assembly, and took the oath of allegiance to his Majesty the King, his heirs and successors. Sufficient repentance this for a frenzied and foolish boycott. He also returned to the Bar. Good men had hoped in vain that Nehru would be his old self again, a mild and sane man.

Nehru's love of leadership drove him against his better judgment to bless and support the threat of independence and non-violent war. He is now going deeper and deeper into the ditch.

The issue in India to-day is peace or war. Old Nehru, with his ragged army, speaks of "war." People laugh at him. He does not inspire the younger men. Nor even his famous son, who is looked upon as a political pendulum!

The real danger, however, comes from those who are not preaching war like these loquacious politicians—they are planning it. The bomb that burst in India's Parliament this year was really a lightning flash of revelation of how beneath the frothy surface of Indian nationalism and Swarajist hypocrisy great forces are silently and dangerously working.

[1] *The Dilemma in India*, pp. 119, 195–197.

CHAPTER XXII

THE DANGER TO INDIA

THE peril to India and to the early solution of her problem arises from the hypocrisy of the Indian politicians on the one side and the bravado of the British agitators on the other.

Nothing within living memory has done greater harm to British reputation in India than the recent criticisms levelled at the Conservative Viceroy, Lord Irwin, by responsible men who ought to have known better, when he made the far-reaching Proclamation about Dominion status. Equally immense is the injury to Britain's name caused by the hysterical repudiation of Indian aspirations by men who were a party to the Montagu pledge.

In a warning issued to Lord Irwin, whose name Lord Birkenhead himself had commended to the Prime Minister and the King for his appointment as the Viceroy and Governor-General of India, the erstwhile Secretary of State for India observed: [1]

> The looseness and vagueness of the language employed are obvious.
>
> What is Dominion status?
>
> Is it what it was before the last Imperial Conference or as it is to-day?
>
> Are the readers of this declaration intended to infer that the "natural goal" of the steps already taken is to produce a system under which the Viceroy will discharge functions comparable to those of the Governor-General of Canada?
>
> Is it intended to convey that the "natural goal" is to produce a system in which the police and military control

[1] *The Daily Telegraph*, London, November 2, 1929.

of Indian conditions will assume a Canadian or Australian complexion?

Every one who knows anything about India plainly realizes that there is no period of time humanly foreseeable in which these changes will be possible without producing in India on an even graver scale the disruptive and anarchical conditions which prevail in China to-day. The language, therefore, used by the Viceroy, on the authority of the Government, either adds something to the declaration of August 1917, or it does not.

When I read this article from the pen of Lord Birkenhead I wondered how he, of all persons, could have made that amazing statement. Speaking in his capacity as the Secretary of State for India in the House of Lords on July 7, 1925, Lord Birkenhead himself had observed:

> We no longer talk of holding the gorgeous East in fee; we invite, in a contrary sense, the diverse peoples of this continent to march side by side with us in a fruitful and harmonious partnership, which may recreate the greatest and the proudest days of Indian history.

The "partnership" of which Lord Birkenhead, his Majesty's Secretary of State, spoke in 1925 is repudiated by Lord Birkenhead, the free-lance, in 1929!

That it is not a reckless outburst in which Lord Birkenhead indulged, but a careful, premeditated statement, is borne out by the fact that in equally forcible and equally cruel style he completely denied India's right to self-government when he said in the House of Lords:

> Dominion *status*! What does Dominion *status* mean? Does it mean that the Viceroy shall decline to a position comparable to that of a Governor-General of Canada, of Australia, of New Zealand? Yet that is an inseparable element in Dominion *status*. . . . No man has a right to indicate to the Indian people that they are likely in any near period to attain to Dominion *status* who does not believe that within a near period they will be capable of assuming the same degree of

control over their Army, Navy, and Civil Service that is assumed by the self-governing Dominions to-day. What man in this House can say that he can see in a generation, in two generations, in a hundred years, any prospect that the people of India will be in a position to assume control of the Army, the Navy, the Civil Service, and to have a Governor-General who will be responsible to the Indian Government and not to any authority in this country?

The above sentiments of Lord Birkenhead have been endorsed by two of his colleagues in the last Conservative Government, Mr Winston Churchill and Lord Brentford. Lord Brentford wrote in a Sunday paper as follows: [1]

> I entirely agree with the views expressed by Lord Birkenhead in his letter to *The Daily Telegraph* regarding the implications in the Viceroy's declaration, made with the sanction of the Government and without consultation with the Simon Commission.
>
> I am one of those who feel that the grant of Dominion Home Rule to India will not only be injurious to British interests, but will be absolutely disastrous to India itself.
>
> The grant of Dominion Home Rule will lead, I am satisfied, to a further demand for complete independence. This, in fact, has already begun. As soon as our control ceases and our Army leaves India the whole place will be a ruin of bloodshed and chaos.
>
> I do not say this without serious thought, but with a certain personal knowledge of India itself.
>
> As a Conservative, I hope neither the party nor its leaders will feel themselves bound by this declaration made by the Viceroy and the Government on their own responsibility. Members of Parliament in both Houses are bound to consider this matter in the light of the interests both of India and of the Empire at large.

Writing in a leading daily paper,[2] Mr Winston Churchill remarked:

[1] *The Sunday Graphic*, November 3, 1929.
[2] *The Daily Mail*, November 16, 1929.

> It is the duty of public men and of political parties to make it plain without delay that the extension of Dominion status to India is not practicable at the present time, and that any attempt to secure it will encounter the earnest resistance of the British nation. There is no need, indeed, we have no right, to close the long avenues of the future; but the idea that Home Rule for India or Dominion status or full responsible government for India can emerge from anything that is now being done or inquired into is not only fantastic in itself, but criminally mischievous in its effects.

The views of Lords Birkenhead and Brentford and of Mr Winston Churchill are shared by the leaders of the Liberal Party.

Lord Reading, in his attack on Lord Irwin's declaration in the House of Lords on November 5, 1929, said: [1]

> My great objection to it (the Viceroy's declaration) is that it has conjured up a picture in India which cannot be fulfilled within a considerable time at least, and that the obstacles remain as they were before this announcement was made, still confronting India.

A Radical in his attitude toward India, who has always doubted the wisdom of Parliamentary intervention in Indian administration, and who does not approve of the existence, for instance, of the Joint Committee of both Houses dealing with Indian affairs, even the Marquess of Crewe endorsed the point of view to which Lord Birkenhead had given expression. The noble Marquess, who took part in the Indian debate in the House of Lords on November 5, 1929, said: [2]

> As can be seen from the debate, so far as it has proceeded, practically the sole objection taken from this side of the House turns on the question of the use of the term "Dominion *status*." The noble and learned Earl, Lord Birkenhead, dealt very fully, and as I thought most fairly, with the use of that

[1] *House of Lords Debates*, Tuesday, November 5, 1929, pp. 380, 381.
[2] *Ibid.*

expression. To me it has always been a matter of deep regret that the term has ever been used in relation to India, and for more reasons than one. . . . But on the question of the use of the words "Dominion *status*," a great number of years ago Sir George Cornewall Lewis, who was one of the clearest thinkers of the nineteenth century, drew attention to the danger which arises from the prevalent habit in this country of applying the same name to political institutions which exist in different parts of the Empire under wholly different conditions. That, as it seems to me, is precisely the danger that you are running now. Because, as we all know—and one might name twenty instances, but I name one—the existence of the Indian States of the Indian Princes creates a state of affairs so entirely different from that which obtains in any other part of the Empire that it is impossible to speak of Dominion *status* for India without explanation, without a great number of mental reservations which you would find it too long to explain. But, unluckily, those who hear the phrase used do not make any of those reservations. As has already been pointed out, they all assume that the use of the words "Dominion *status*" means some early approximation of the Government of India to the Governments of the great self-governing Dominions, such as Canada, Australia, and South Africa. And the term "Dominion," as we all know, came into use because the term "Colony" was felt to be inapplicable to these great self-governing communities.

It is that misunderstanding, that evident misunderstanding, of which proof has been given in the extracts which noble Lords have read, which has caused us our present anxiety.

We have seen the agreement, from the above quotation, of a Radical with the Conservative Lord Birkenhead.

It would be sufficient for our purpose to say that Mr Lloyd George, whose Government, when he was the Prime Minister, pledged Britain to the Montagu policy, felt constrained to repudiate it in words which have staggered India. Mr Lloyd George said in the House of Commons on November 7, 1929: [1]

[1] Hansard, vol. 231, p. 1316.

After the War, or, *rather, during the War, there was a very deep sense of gratitude to India for the great and loyal support of all its peoples in a very great emergency.* . . . There was also the impulse of the dominating cry throughout the world about self-determination. These were the conditions in which we considered the question of self-government for India.

Now that the memory of India's service in the War is fading, the politicians in England, separated from India by more than half the world and alive only to their own selfish interest in the exploitation of that great country by keeping her in permanent bondage, have the audacity to turn back on Britain's pledge to India. "Gratitude," of which Mr Lloyd George spoke, is hardly a political virtue!

England, which was grateful to India " during the War," is, I still believe, grateful. If any party were to make Home Rule for India its election cry there is no doubt whatever that the great English democracy will vote for Indian Home Rule. But England is different from the English or British politician.

The politician is not—to whatever party he may belong, Labour not excepted—willing to grant Home Rule to India. Though that was the definite purpose of Mr Montagu's policy, which was approved by Mr Lloyd George's Government "after the War or, rather, during the War," that certainly does not seem to be the present purpose of Parliament. So high an authority as the Viceroy of India, himself a Conservative, expressed to the Secretary of State for India his own doubts and the suspicions of the people of India about Britain's *bona fides* in regard to a pledge granted to India by Parliament and endorsed by the King in his gracious message through his Royal Highness the Duke of Connaught, who went out to India to inaugurate the new era of democracy.[1]

[1] "For years, it may be for generations, patriotic and loyal Indians have dreamed of *Swaraj* for their Motherland. To-day you have beginnings of *Swaraj* within my Empire; and widest scope and ample opportunity for progress to the liberty which my other *Dominions* enjoy."—Message of his Majesty the King-Emperor, delivered by the Duke of Connaught on February 9, 1921.

The Viceroy, who came to England on a special mission, informed the Secretary of State for India, in the words of Mr Wedgwood Benn,

> in the first place, that doubts had arisen in India as to the sincerity of British parties in the matter of the Montagu policy. Does anybody doubt that of recent years there had grown up a feeling, and it had constantly been said, that British policy was altering, that the tone was altering, that sympathy was gone, that the days of Mr Montagu were past. The Viceroy said that these doubts existed, and that for the removal of these doubts it was necessary to issue a clear declaration of existing policy. We did so. The second reason he gave was this. He said, " The Statutory Commission is going to report, and we want if we can to make a good atmosphere for the Report. We want to have an atmosphere of good will, and that will be better secured if we can clear up the doubts which exist in the minds of Indians who have been assisting the British Government and co-operating with us and helping the work of the Montagu schemes, and remove the webs of mistrust which it is necessary to clear away." That was the purpose and these were the reasons alleged by the Viceroy and given to the Cabinet as reasons why we should take this course, and it was because those reasons appeared to us to be good and sound that the Government took the course which they did take.[1]

The Secretary of State for India further declared : " *The Montagu policy stands as a cardinal article of faith in British policy.*"

But Mr Lloyd George thinks Mr Montagu's policy was not to grant Dominion status to India as interpreted by Lord Irwin the Viceroy and approved by his Majesty's Government ! Mr Lloyd George definitely wanted to defeat the purpose of the Viceroy and the Government of India when he said : [2]

> What has happened? The Viceroy comes over to this

[1] House of Commons debate on November 7, 1929 (Hansard, vol. 231, pp. 1321, 1322).
[2] *Ibid.*

country, a thing almost without precedent,[1] during his term of office. He comes here, and it is known, to consult the Government and leaders of public opinion here with regard to what is going to happen. It is announced that a very important deliverance is going to be made by him as soon as he returns to India. Is it conceivable to English public opinion, not only to Indians, that he is going to make a declaration merely that there is no change, merely repeating what has been said before by previous Viceroys, and that there is no change at all in substance or in time? Indian opinion naturally thought that this was a great deliverance, and portended a very startling change of policy.

The fears of Lord Birkenhead, Messrs Lloyd George, Reading, and Co. were set at rest when Lords Parmoor and Passfield, speaking for the Government in the House of Lords, said that there was no idea on the part of the Socialist Government to accelerate, much less to precipitate, the grant of Dominion status to India; that, alike in the point of time and space, there was no change of policy.

Mr Wedgwood Benn, however, struck a different note in the House of Commons when he declared:[2] "*The first change has been a change of spirit.* We have got rid of the Birkenhead tone. . . ."[3]

With due respect to the Right Hon. Wedgwood Benn, "the Birkenhead tone" was, though not just the same as his own when Lord Birkenhead was the Secretary of State for India, more sympathetic and earnest than the new tone he has adopted in an unofficial—and therefore irresponsible—position. Lord Birkenhead, however, speaks with that refreshing candour which must be welcome to

[1] There was a precedent. Lord Irwin's predecessor, Lord Reading, the Liberal Viceroy, came home during his term of office, though confronted with a less serious crisis.

[2] Debate on November 7, 1929 (Hansard, vol. 231, p. 1322).

[3] What about the Russell tone? Earl Russell, who is the Parliamentary Under-Secretary of State for India, recently made a speech on India at Cambridge in which he surpassed Lord Birkenhead. Well might Lord Birkenhead congratulate Earl Russell on his candid utterance on India in *The Daily Telegraph* of January 17.

India, because it is stripped of the camouflage of official verbiage, which Socialist Ministers have learned to use like their Tory predecessors!

Though the tone and general attitude of the Labour Government and of Mr Wedgwood Benn appear more conciliatory, has there been any change in their programme, principle, or policy? Mr Wedgwood Benn says yes, and his Prime Minister and Government's spokesmen in the House of Lords say no.

Mr Wedgwood Benn says:

> *The first change that is made is a change of spirit, but the second is far more important: it is a change in policy*, which in reality is the central object of interest in Indian opinion, and that is the Conference.

The Prime Minister, in a formal letter to Mr Baldwin, denied that there was a change of policy, either in regard to the time or measure, about the grant of Dominion status to India. This formal repudiation of the Secretary of State by his chief—which might have led to resignation if the latter had really decided to impart a new spirit and embark on a new policy—has satisfied even so thorough an opponent of Indian Home Rule as Mr Winston Churchill, who wrote: [1]

> What is the purpose and meaning of this new declaration?
>
> The formal letter which Mr Baldwin has drawn from the Prime Minister by his direct questions has given an answer as clear and explicit as the English language can convey.
>
> The Viceroy's declaration, we are assured, involves no new departure from the preamble of the Act of Parliament of 1919.

Thus the Viceregal Proclamation has been whittled down with the approval of the Prime Minister of the Socialist Government. All that remains is the offer of a Round Table Conference, which has not been formally withdrawn!

Whether the Conference meets or not matters not. The hypocrisy of the Indian leaders—and the temptation of a

[1] *The Daily Mail*, November 16, 1929.

voyage to England at Government's expense—will induce them to come to England. But what will be the ultimate outcome? Those who come to confer with the Government on Indian Home Rule will go back and tell their countrymen, "England has cheated us. Englishmen do not propose to give India Home Rule."

At the best, the Nehrus and other alleged extremists like Speaker Patel will accept cushy jobs under the Simon dispensation and work the reforms. They will, in other words, become good boys and settle down to a sensible existence. Then they will be discredited and thrown down from their present position of exalted leadership. For it must be clearly understood that the movement for freedom has come to stay in India. It does not depend on this leader or that. Men may come and men may go, but the Freedom-for-India movement will move on until the goal is reached.

England can reduce India's ideal of freedom to "Dominion *status*" if she immediately prepares India for self-defence by opening a military college in every big province in India equal to Britain in size and population—"to recreate," in Lord Birkenhead's words, "the greatest and the proudest days of Indian history." [1]

Indian boys have been denied adequate opportunities for an Army career. The unanimous recommendations of the Indian Sandhurst Committee, presided over by Sir Andrew Skeen, suggesting the establishment of one military college in India—whereas every province ought to have an Indian Sandhurst—have been shelved. England will have immediately to revise this attitude [2] if she means to fulfil the pledge of Dominion status given in the fullness of her "gratitude during the War." If England does not propose

[1] Speech in the House of Lords, July 7, 1925.

[2] "No man has a right to indicate to the Indian people that they are likely in any near period to attain to Dominion *status* who does not believe that within a near period they will be capable of assuming the same degree of control over their Army, Navy, and Civil Service that is assumed by the self-governing Dominions to-day."—Lord Birkenhead in the House of Lords on November 5, 1929 (*House of Lords Debates*, vol. 75, p. 403).

to revise the age-old policy of distrusting India and denying her opportunities for Home Defence—without which there can be no Home Rule—she must be prepared for ever-growing mistrust in India, which will finally goad her into a revolution.

India has been a nation of worms. She has been trampled underfoot for ages by alien conquerors. But even a trampled worm will turn unless completely crushed. *India cannot be crushed.* The worm is turning!

Must India become an Ireland, a hundredfold more dangerous, because she is so far away from England and so much vaster in size and population? Ireland could be saved for England, partly because of their common British stock and other ties between Englishmen and Irishmen—and the fact of their being neighbours—but once India, which has no such relations, rises and revolts, she cannot be saved. It may be that she may pass under some other foreign conqueror. It may be that she may split up into independent Provinces, forming independent nations. It may be that she may be plunged into anarchy, worse than the worst civil war known to history or humanity. If England wants to save India from anarchy England must give up her politicians' petty policy of saying one thing and unsaying it the next moment, of making a promise in words and breaking it in deeds.

India is preparing for the attainment of self-government. With England's assent it can be the happy culmination of a peaceful evolution, admitting of two or three easy stages to which even the most dangerous extremist will agree to-day:

First, Provincial autonomy and simultaneous substantial responsibility in the Central Government.

Secondly, Home Rule in British India, including control of the Army.

Thirdly, Dominion status for the whole of India—*i.e.*, British India and the Native States—under the control of a Central All-Indian Supreme Parliament.

If England is not prepared to grant the first stage forthwith, and earnestly begin preparations for the second and the third stages, she must be prepared for trouble and more trouble, beginning with India's boycott of British goods, leading to an early economic collapse, bringing untold hardships to countless numbers in both India and England, and culminating in repeated efforts at a complete overthrow of the British *Raj* in India. The true extremist exclaims, in language the significance of which cannot be lost on England:

> Hereditary bondsmen! Know ye not
> Who would be free themselves must strike the blow?

England can yet save India for the Empire by following the example set in regard to South Africa by one of her great statesmen, Sir Henry Campbell-Bannerman, who truly said, "Good government can be no substitute for self-government."

In his happiest vein Mr Stanley Baldwin gave expression to these romantic facts of history: [1]

> Far away in time, in the dawn of history, the greatest race of the many races then emerging from prehistoric mists was the great Aryan race. When that race left the country which it occupied in the western branch of Central Asia, one great branch moved west, and in the course of their wanderings they founded the cities of Athens and Sparta; they founded Rome; they made Europe, and in the veins of the principal nations of Europe flows the blood of their Aryan forefathers. The speech of the Aryans which they brought with them has spread throughout Europe. It has spread to America. It has spread to the Dominions beyond the seas. At the same time, one branch went south, and they crossed the Himalayas. They went into the Punjab and they spread through India, and, as an historic fact, ages ago, there stood side by side in their ancestral land the ancestors of the English people and the ancestors of the Rajputs and of the Brahmins. And now,

[1] Speech in the House of Commons, November 7, 1929 (Hansard, pp. 1307, 1308).

> after æons have passed, the children of the remotest generations from that ancestry have been brought together by the inscrutable decree of Providence to set themselves to solve the most difficult, the most complicated, political problem that has ever been set to any people of the world.

Britain cannot be unaware of the march of events in India. She must understand the hunger for freedom ; it accords with the best British traditions ; it is in line with the highest human aspirations. She is also alive to her own interests, commercial and Imperial, which stand to gain if India is conciliated and contented. A contented India will also be the bridge with which England can span the gulf that yawns between East and West.

If England only realizes it, she has a mission in India: she will lead that vast and wonderful country to take her place in the comity of nations. And the day is not distant when India, self-governing and free, equal partner of an Indo-British Commonwealth, the greatest democracy the world has seen, hand in hand with Britain, will contribute to the peaceful solution of the problem of the human race, when East will aid the understanding West to banish all wars, aggressions, and usurpations, and salute the golden dawn of everlasting world-peace!

POSTSCRIPT

SINCE the foregoing pages were written some events have occurred, a cursory mention of which cannot be omitted.

The evening papers in London on December 23, 1929, published the staggering news of an attempt to assassinate Lord Irwin, the Viceroy, and Lady Irwin, and to wreck the special train in which their Excellencies travelled. On the same day, in the House of Commons, his Majesty's Secretary of State for India read the following message from the Viceroy to the King:

> I regret to have to inform your Majesty that an attempt was made this morning to wreck my train by exploding a bomb under it as we were approaching Delhi. Luckily no harm was done, and few of us realized what had occurred. I hope your Majesty therefore will not be disturbed by exaggerated reports.

According to the special correspondent of *The Times* at Delhi:

> Lord Irwin's arrival as the first Viceroy to enter Delhi to-day [December 23] was marred by a plot against his life which failed only by the merest chance. A bomb exploded under the Viceregal train within three miles of New Delhi Railway Station, with the result that two carriages were badly damaged, a section of the rail more than two feet long was blown away, and a sleeper was smashed to splinters. The fact that complete disaster to the train, involving its fall down a thirty-foot embankment, did not follow is inexplicable to those who, like myself, have seen the shattered carriages and damaged line.
>
> The exact point where the attempt was made was on a single track which runs on the embankment within two hundred yards of the Purana Kila, the historic fortress built

by Sher Shah in the sixteenth century. Here a heavy bomb was planted between the rails under the edge of a sleeper. A length of insulated wire ran two hundred yards to a spot at the foot of the greystone bastion marking the corner of the fort walls. This was connected with a battery, about six inches square, which is now in the hands of the police. The wire was buried over its full length about two inches deep, and there is every sign that the crime was not only carefully planned and premeditated, but was carried out by persons having much scientific skill.

Punctually at 7.40 the white carriages of the Viceroy's train appeared out of the heavy mists shrouding the country. It was travelling at between thirty and forty miles an hour, and would have been going more quickly but for the fog. As the train reached a spot opposite the conspirators the button was pressed, and the bomb exploded under the passage connecting the second and third coaches. The second coach was the dining-car and the third the stenographer's office. The flooring of the passage rose in the shape of an arch. The steelwork was twisted, and the planks were splintered.

When I saw the spot a few minutes later a large triangular piece of the bomb, firmly embedded in the roof after having passed through the flooring, bore witness to the strength of the explosion. The heavy plate-glass windows in the dining-car and the third coach were shattered to fragments. The fourth coach, in which the staff was travelling, was untouched. The fifth coach, which was the Viceroy's, was so little affected that Lord Irwin did not realize what had happened until told by his Military Secretary. In the fourth coach the noise of the explosion sounded like a fog-signal. A moment later there was a fairly severe bump, but it was only when smoke fumes came drifting down the passage that it was realized something was wrong. An Indian bearer clearing up in the dining-car was knocked over by the shock and slightly injured, but nobody else was hurt.

Even more astonishing than the escape from the bomb itself was the escape from derailment. This afternoon I walked from the foot of the fort, where the conspirators had lain in hiding, along the line of buried wire (which ran through broken, heavily wooded country), climbed the steep embankment, and saw the shattered rail and sleeper. The rail was broken clean off at the flange, and the sleeper looked like a bundle of firewood. How the remaining coaches, one after another, jumped the gap without leaving the rails is difficult to understand. Derailment would have caused a plunge down the embankment, as there are only a few feet of clearance on either side of the line.

A few minutes later the train pulled into New Delhi Station. Lord Irwin, who was completely unperturbed, shook hands with officials and entered his car for the drive to the Viceroy's House.

Seventeen years ago a similar attempt was made on the life of Lord Hardinge, the Viceroy, on his State entry to the new capital.

The attempt to assassinate Lord Irwin must have been the work of the revolutionary gang who do not believe in India's coming to an understanding with Britain; who do not believe Dominion status will be granted by Britain; and who rely on the use of force to win their country's freedom.

Both Indian constitutionalists and British opinion have condemned the bomb outrage. The outrage is quite definitely an attempt on the part of the revolutionaries to avert a compromise in regard to the question of Dominion status. Indian leaders have unequivocally denounced the action of those who were at the bottom of the conspiracy.

It would be useful to note what the organs of the British Press have to say on the depressing news from India on Christmas Eve.

The Morning Post (December 24) says that

> the Delhi bomb outrage, to be frank, must be laid at the door of those statesmen, in the East and at Westminster, who imagine that we can govern native races by surrendering our authority to a clique of native *intelligentsia.*

This is a rather absurd view to take. But for the progressive policy of reforms the constitutional leaders would not have come forward to oppose the revolutionary movement. There would then have been only one force—the bomb. It was such a dangerous crisis that Lord Irwin tried to avert —or at any rate postpone—by his conciliatory declaration. The bomb incident is an evidence of the exasperation of the revolutionaries as their hold on the country is diminishing and the prestige of the loyal co-operating Indians and of Britain in the past is increasing. The best friends of the bomb-thrower in India are Tory Die-hards like *The Morning Post*.

The Daily Mail says: [1]

> Sir John Simon, the head of the Commission, whose judgment on the state of India we are now awaiting, has himself been nearly involved in an equally wicked and murderous attempt. We hold that it would be criminal folly to commit the high responsibility of Dominion status to a country where political feuds can still be prosecuted by these barbarous methods.

War is admittedly "a barbarous method," but to deny to a whole country its just due because there are in it bands of fanatics is neither English nor human. And British history shows that Britain is not influenced by such outbreaks to turn her back upon her great mission.

Lord Irwin himself was not affected by the tragic occurrence. Within an hour of the attempt to assassinate him the Viceroy was replying to an address from the new Delhi municipality and referring to "the labours of those whose task it will be under Providence to achieve the full destiny of India among the Dominions of the Empire."

Later in the afternoon Lord Irwin met at his residence five Indian Nationalist leaders—Mr Gandhi, Pundit Motilal Nehru, Mr Patel,[2] Mr Jinnah, and Sir Tej Sapru—who had written asking for an invitation to place before him their

[1] The quotations are all from the morning papers of December 24, 1929.

[2] Speaker Patel should not have been in that political deputation. The Speaker has no politics.

views on the recent announcement regarding a proposed Round Table Conference on the future constitution of India.

Well might *The Daily Telegraph* say with a legitimate sense of satisfaction:

> The Viceroy has been the first to demonstrate that the bloodthirsty insanity of a band of Communist thugs cannot affect the development of British policy in dealing with the quite separate issue of constitutional reform. With unshaken coolness, he proceeded to the prearranged meeting at Viceroy's House with the most influential personalities in the leadership of the National Congress that is to be opened this week in Lahore. The meeting had been awaited with keen interest, if only because it took place at the request of Mr Gandhi and his four colleagues, who thus departed from their long-standing rule of avoiding all personal contacts with the Administration.

All right-minded Englishmen will agree with *The Daily Express*:

> Wise or unwise, timely or premature, the policy to which we have set our hands in India is not to be deflected by violence aimed at least as much against the Indian moderates as against the British *Raj*.

The opinion of *The Daily Herald* is valuable as reflecting the policy of the Government:

> The object of the fanatic who attempted to murder Lord Irwin, his wife, and his staff on their way to Delhi is only too evident. The terrorists are filled with panic fear at the possibility of a peaceful negotiation and an ultimate settlement between the Viceroy and the Indian political leaders. And they are determined to use every means. . . .

The Daily Herald further observes:

> Fortunately, neither Mr Benn nor Lord Irwin is of the type to be stampeded into coercive folly either by crime or by the cry for vengeance. Never was a moment when there was more need for cool thinking and for clear resolves.

POSTSCRIPT

The Daily Chronicle speaks the whole truth when it reflects how all sane Indians rejoice with England in the Viceroy's escape:

> The murderous attempt to wreck the train on which the Viceroy of India was travelling yesterday has called forth the same expressions of horror in India as it evokes in this country. The brutal argument of assassination recoils on the heads of those who resort to it. Even extremists in India see that their cause can only be discredited when one of their number uses so dastardly a weapon; the more so as in this case the person against whom it was directed is so deeply respected and beloved as Lord Irwin.

Britain is not obviously going to grant immediately what the extremist wants. But is she prepared to grant the demands of the Loyalists? The Report of the Joint Central Committee of the Indian Legislature, who declined to boycott the Simon Commission, with whom they wholeheartedly collaborated, has just been published. This Report does not demand immediate Dominion status, like Gandhi and the Congress. It wants a definite preparation of India from now for Dominion status. The Report, besides demanding the abolition of dyarchy in the provinces, says:

> There exists in India a very widespread belief that the British Government has no real intention of ever allowing the people of India to obtain genuine self-government; that the Army will continue to be maintained as a weapon in the hands of the British Government for the retention of India in subjection; and that the alleged unfitness of Indians for high command will continue to be put forward as an argument against the final handing over into Indian hands of responsibility for the government of the country.
>
> It is, in our opinion, of the utmost importance that the British Government should lose no further time in affording to the people of India definite proofs that such suspicions are unwarranted.
>
> The grant to provincial governments of the right to raise

a local army for the maintenance of internal security would be a long step in this direction. . . . The majority of us accordingly recommend that it should be open to the Governments of Madras and Bombay to equip and maintain a local military force and a local militia.

On the subject of the Army in India, the Committee take the view that it is unfair to make India's advance conditional on the ability to undertake her defence, while she is denied full opportunity to do so, and they ask that she should be allowed to man the Indian portion of the army " by her own sons " as a preliminary to taking over the whole work of the defence of the country.

" In our opinion, there is no safe half-way house between dyarchy and full responsibility," declare the Committee, and they describe India's minimum demands in the following terms :

(1) An explicit declaration on the part of the British Government that full Dominion status for India be the goal at which it aims.

(2) That an immediate and substantial step should be taken toward the attainment of that goal by the conferring on the provinces of a liberal measure of autonomy, and by making the Government of India responsible to its Legislature in accordance with our detailed recommendations.

(3) That provision should be made in the Government of India Act which will enable the above goal to be reached without the necessity for further inquiries by statutory commissions or other agency.

The Committee say they are convinced that there is no safe half-way house between an immediate advance on the lines indicated in their report and an ultimate surrender by the British Government after years of agitation and bitterness to India's insistent demand.

They believe that this " may be the *last opportunity* that a British Government will ever have of rallying to its side all the saner and more responsible elements of Indian opinion and of strengthening their hand against the forces of disorder." [1]

Such is the report of his Majesty's Indian Commissioners. They courageously courted "the immortality of censure," as Manu said. They went against several old friends and colleagues when they co-operated with the British Commission. They defied the defiance of their own people, who cried cruel shame on them wherever they went. They are loyal, proud of their loyalty to the Throne, staunch in their friendship to Britain, and extremely temperate in language and aspiration. When they fear that this is the last opportunity their apprehension must have a good foundation. A *last* opportunity displays its forelock in front as it passes, but a *lost* opportunity displays the bald on the back. This baldness is an eternal grin at bankrupt statesmanship!

There is a tide in the affairs of nations which taken at the flood leads on to peace and power.

[1] *Report of the Joint Central Committee of the Indian Legislature*, published in 1929 (*His Majesty's Stationery Office*).

INDEX OF NAMES